AF594549

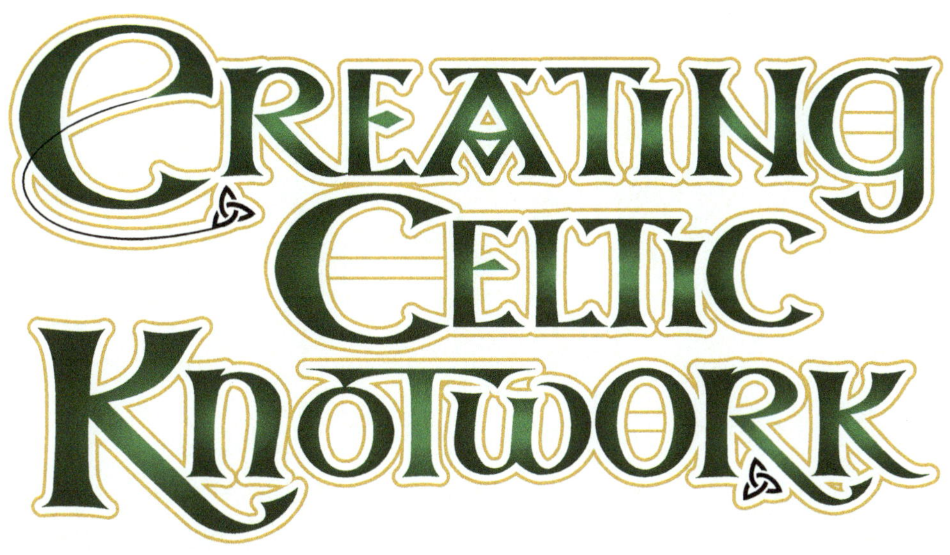

A Fresh Approach to Traditional Design

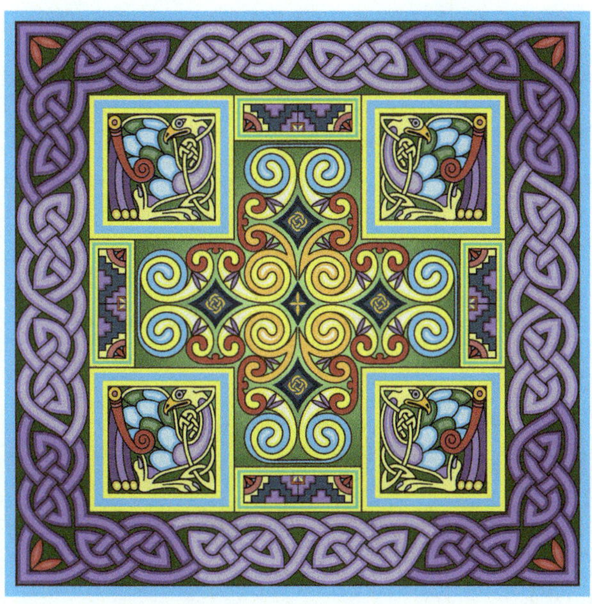

CARI BUZIAK

Dover Publications
Garden City, New York

Creating Celtic Knotwork: A Fresh Approach to Traditional Design
is a new work, first published by Dover Publications in 2018.

Library of Congress Cataloging-in-Publication Data
Names: Buziak, Cari, author.
Title: Creating Celtic knotwork : a fresh approach to traditional design / Cari Buziak.
Description: Garden City, New York : Dover Publications, [2018]
Identifiers: LCCN 2017034178| ISBN 9780486820330 | ISBN 0486820335
Subjects: LCSH: Knotwork, Celtic. | Drawing—Technique.
Classification: LCC NK1264 .B89 2018 | DDC 746.44028—dc23
LC record available at https://lccn.loc.gov/2017034178

Printed in Canada
82033504 2025
www.doverpublications.com

Acknowledgments

This book is dedicated to my dad and my sister.

I love you both very much!

Contents

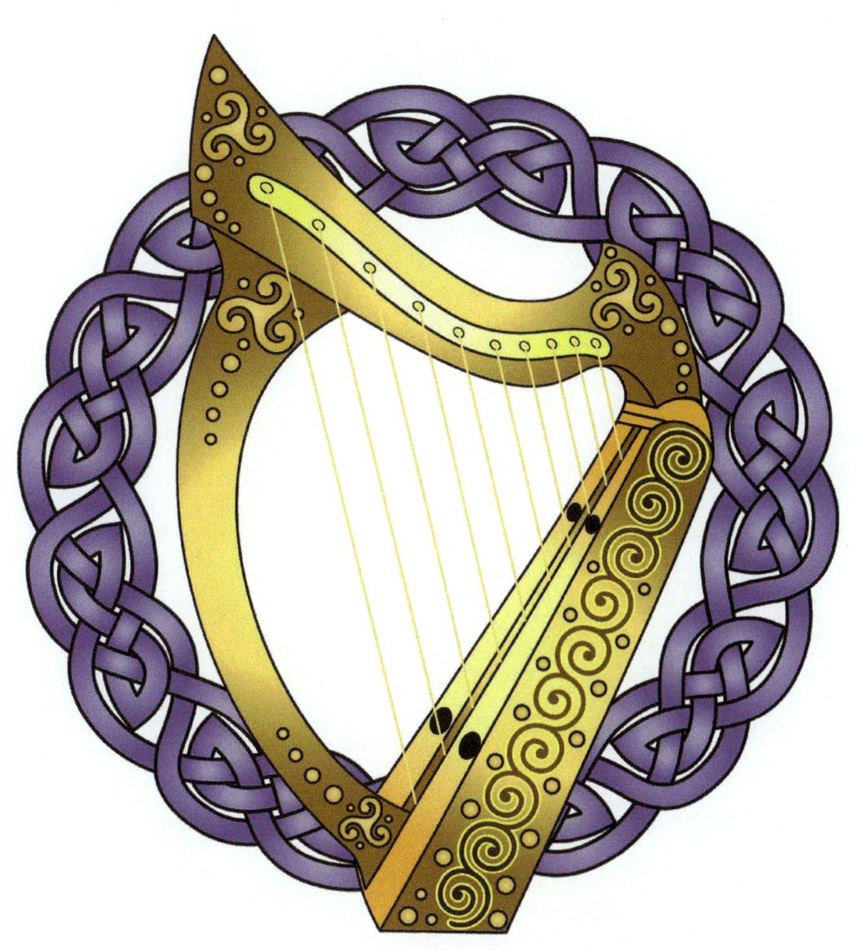

The Basics

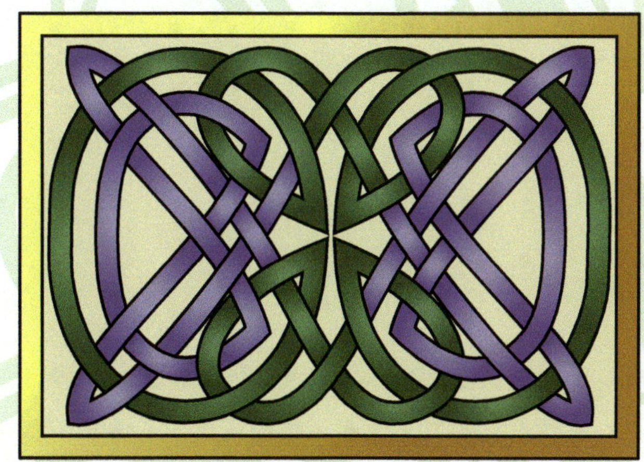

Getting Ready...

To create Celtic knots I use a technique that's based on a gridwork of alternating big and small dots. The dots create a pattern that allows you to make new knotwork designs easily and even in shapes other than just rectangles or squares, as you'll see later in this and other chapters. This book includes a few sheets of ready-made "dot paper" for you, but to create your own is easy.

Tip

Photocopy the sheets in the back of this book before you begin working. That way you'll always have a master page to copy from and won't have to make dotted paper again for each project!

Normal graph paper is made up of a series of squares all over the page. You can sometimes purchase it with bigger or smaller squares, depending on the size of knot you want to create. If only one size is available it can be scaled up or down using a photocopier, or made from scratch at any size using a computer.

Using different-colored markers or a pen, alternate coloring one big dot, followed by a smaller dot, all across the page of graph paper. Make sure that as you move down to the next row you continue to alternate the dots. If there is a big dot above in the previous row, then below it there should be a small dot, and so on. Once the whole sheet is covered, make a photocopy before using it—that way you won't have to make it again next time.

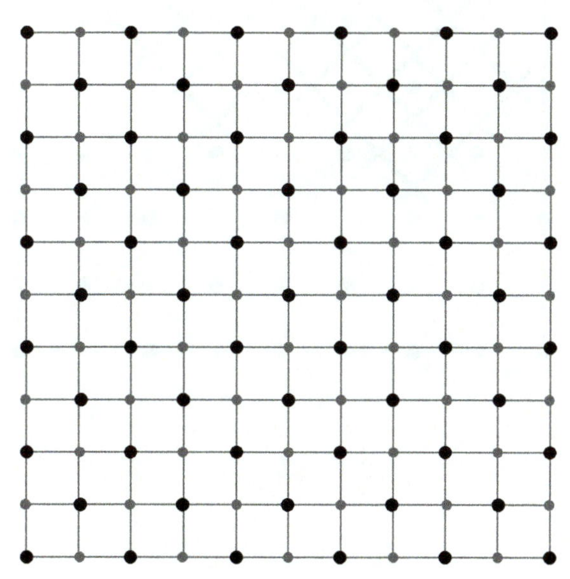

Basic Celtic Knotwork

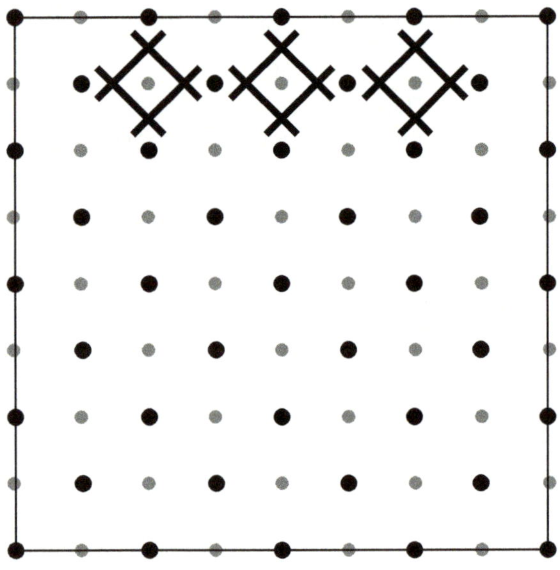

For clarity, in my examples I will display only the big and small dots and not the graph paper lines.

To make your first knot, mark off a box anywhere on the sheet, at least 5 big dots and 4 little dots across. Mark the same distance down (5 big and 4 little dots) so you have an even square. For the dot system to work properly, make sure box corners are always on a BIG dot.

Each small dot is going to be an intersection where two "ropes" of knots are going to cross over each other. Begin to add a double-lined "X" over the little dots within the marked-off box, with each set of the "X" lines running to either side of the little dot like a tic-tac-toe board tipped on its side.

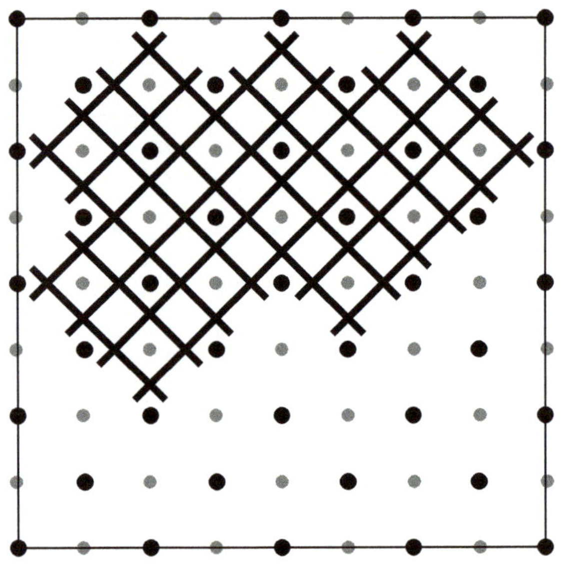

Continue drawing a double-lined "X" over each little dot until reaching the box border. Do not "X" the little dots that lie right on the border line, just those that fall within the border. Your big dots never get crossed over by the knot. Think of the big dots as posts that the knot must bend around to follow its path. You will find that the "X" patterns will meet up on the diagonal, which is correct. If you're making a very large knot, you can make this step go faster by using a ruler and just drawing a line along the diagonal of the little dots. However, when you begin to make very complicated knots, the "X" method keeps things from getting tangled up because it's easier to see clearly what's going on as you proceed.

Basic Celtic Knotwork...

At this point, there should be a double "X" over every little dot in the box. There will be empty spaces along the sides of the box and at the corners, but the center portion should be filled with the "X" pattern, as shown here.

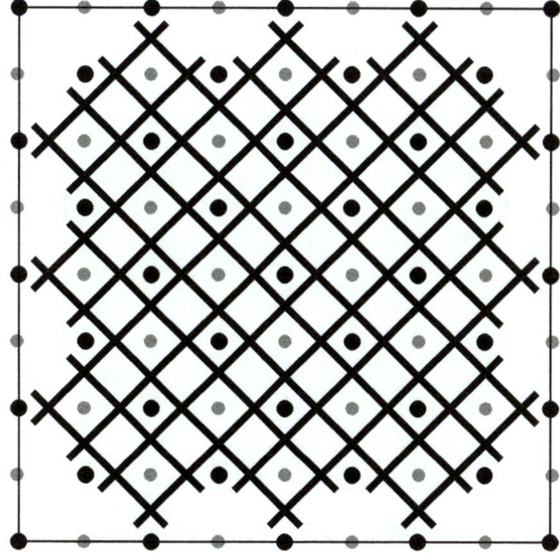

Now that all the little dots are bordered with the "X" pattern, join the knot lines along the sides, top, and bottom of the box. Along one side (it doesn't matter which you begin with) find two pairs of lines angling out toward each other from the body of the "X" pattern. Connect these to each other with a smooth curve. Vary the sharpness of the turn to suit your tastes, from a 90-degree angle to a soft, round curve. There are many variations you can create by varying the angle of the bends.

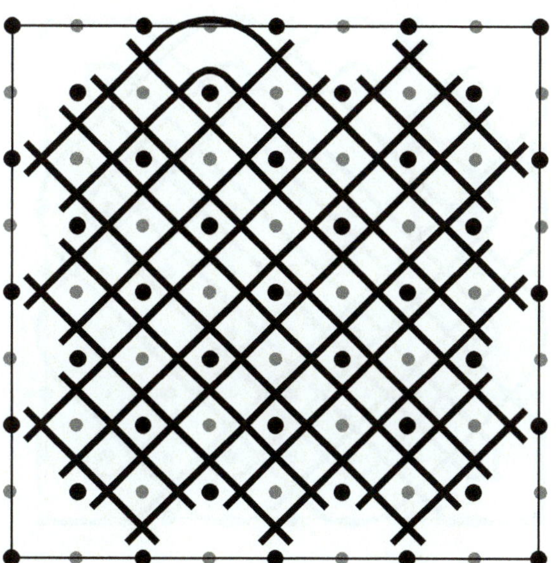

Basic Celtic Knotwork...

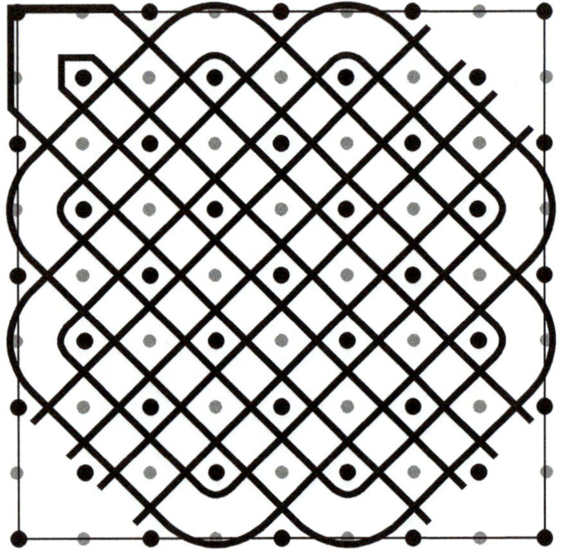

Once all the loose ends that angle toward each other on the sides are joined, add corners. As with the sides, the way you join the corners is up to you, and you may want to experiment with different corners (see the examples on pages 9, 10, 13 and 14).

Joining the corners is easy, as there are only two pairs of lines in each corner to join. If there are other lines left over, then you have probably drawn the marked-off box incorrectly and put a corner on a small dot. Remember, for the pattern to work every corner of the marked-off box must be on a BIG dot. Also, check that you have not added an "X" to any of the small dots on the box border line. That will also break the pattern.

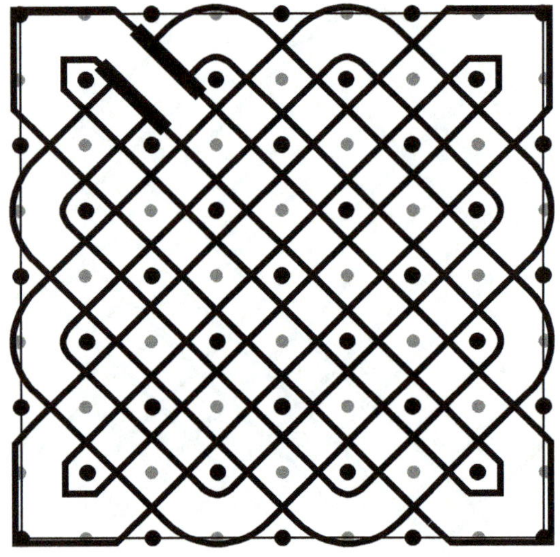

With all the lines connected on the knot we can begin to make the strands weave, or interlace. Each strand, if you follow it with your finger, will be made to appear as though it alternates over and then under and then over any other strand it intersects with. So any strand in the knot will appear to go over-under-over-under the other strands in the knot.

To begin, pick an intersection on the knot over a little dot. It doesn't matter which you choose. Erase part of the double lines, making the illusion that one strand is crossing over the other (see top left of the graph).

Basic Celtic Knotwork...

Trace the path of that same strand of knot. When it reaches the next intersection, erase part of the double lines, but this time change the direction of your erasing—if you erased the first intersection as an over, this next one should be an under, or vice versa. Continue to follow the path, alternating overs and unders as you go. If you reach the beginning and there are still strands of over/under that haven't been erased, don't worry. This just means that your knot actually has more than one strand of knotwork in it. Simply pick an unerased intersection and look at the other ones around it. If the strand leading into the intersection has just come from UNDER another strand, you need to erase your lines so it now passes OVER this one. Continue until all the intersections have been erased.

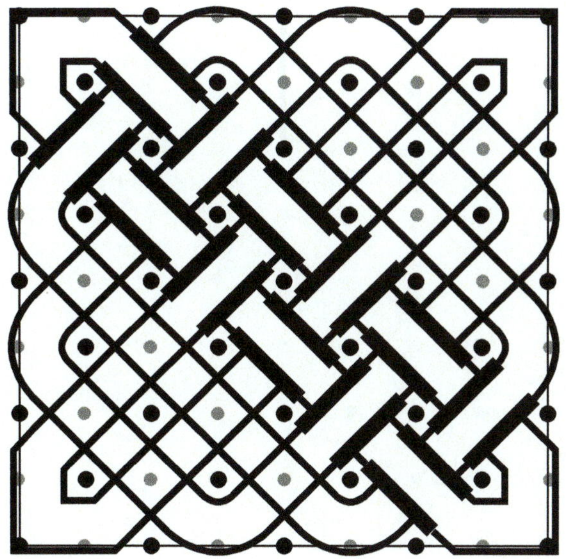

Finished!

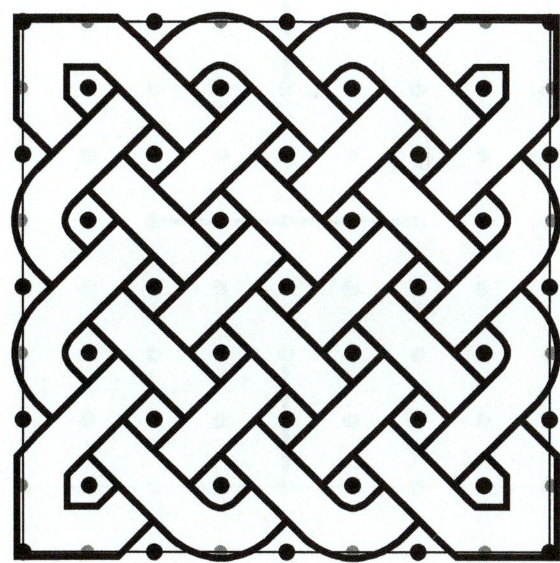

Modifying the Basic Knot

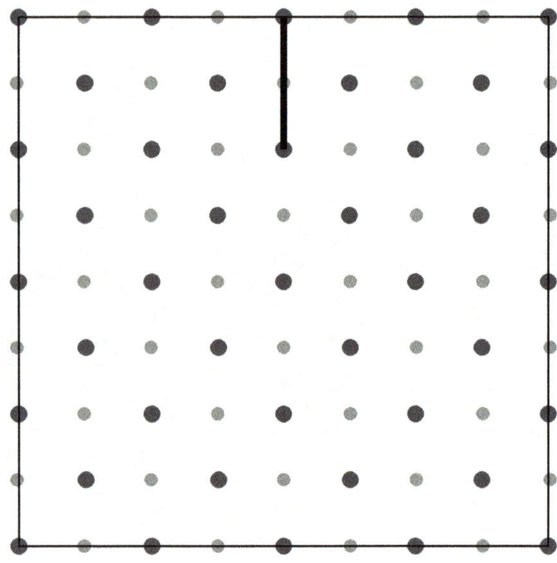

To add complexity to your knotwork, begin the same way we started a Basic Knot. Mark off a portion of your graph paper with 5 big dots and 4 little dots across. Mark the same distance down the graph (5 big and 4 little dots) so it is even. As you already know, each small dot is going to be an intersection where two strands of knot are going to cross over each other, but this time we are going to interrupt their path with "walls," which will force the knot lines to bend in different directions. The walls are placed between two (or more) BIG dots and only lie on the horizontal and/ or vertical. Place these walls anywhere you like.

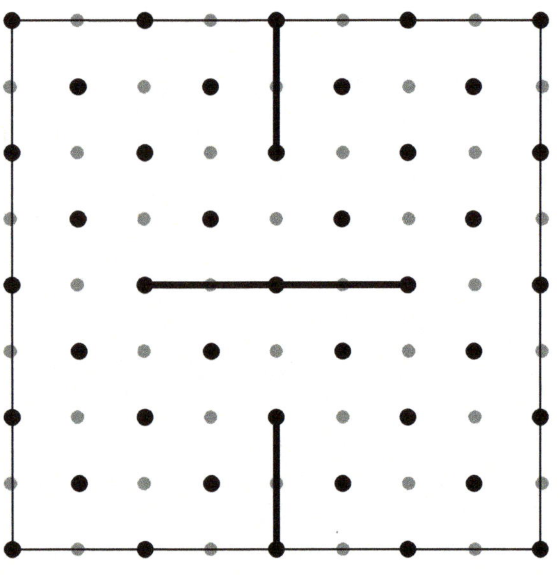

On my example I have marked off two walls jutting out from the top and bottom borders, as well as floated one long wall in the center of my box. Walls may also be placed in combinations when creating your knot. You can line them up several across or partner them up into "T" or "L" or "+" shapes, and each will give you a different knotwork pattern. Always remember to add the walls on the horizontal and vertical (never the diagonal), or your design won't turn out right.

Modifying the Basic Knot...

At this point, start marking your "X" pattern over all the little dots on your graph. Do this over every little dot on the graph EXCEPT for those that have a wall through them. This is where the knot lines are going to be bent away from their paths—because they can't pass through a wall, the lines will bend away naturally into other directions.

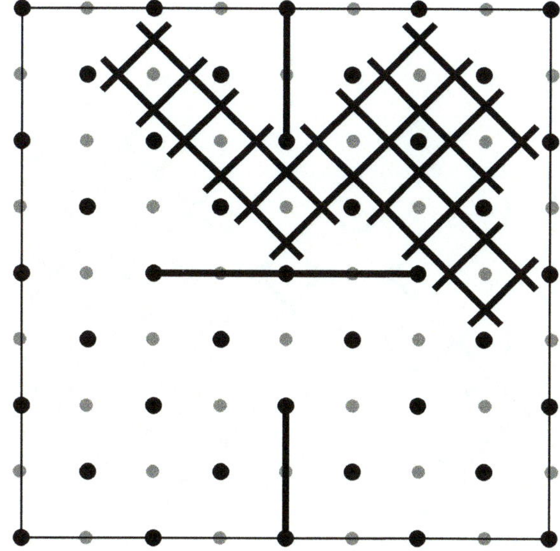

Now your knot should have all the little dots crossed. You can probably already see how the pattern is going to go just by looking at the design. This can be helpful when making a lot of different patterns to fill an entire page, because you can often tell whether there is enough detail and how the design is roughly going to go. At this point, either scrap them if they aren't going to work or add more walls to break up the pattern.

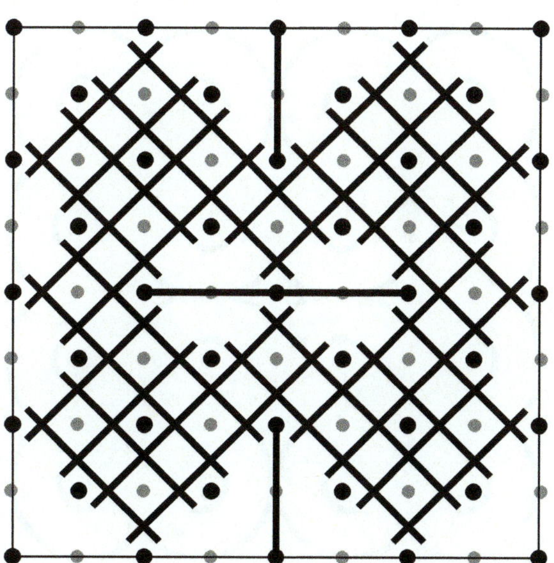

Modifying the Basic Knot...

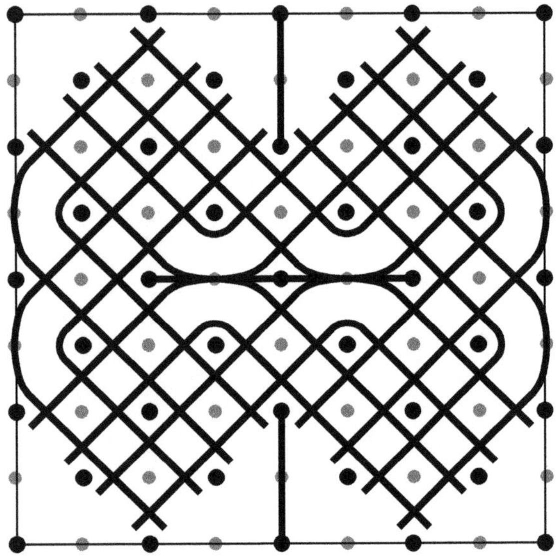

Now check whether the pattern has any bends along the walls or boundary box outlines. As with the basic knot, these lines will be angled toward each other.

Notice in the example how at no time do the knot strands pass over the walls. They're forced to bounce off of them or bend around them—this is how the pattern develops.

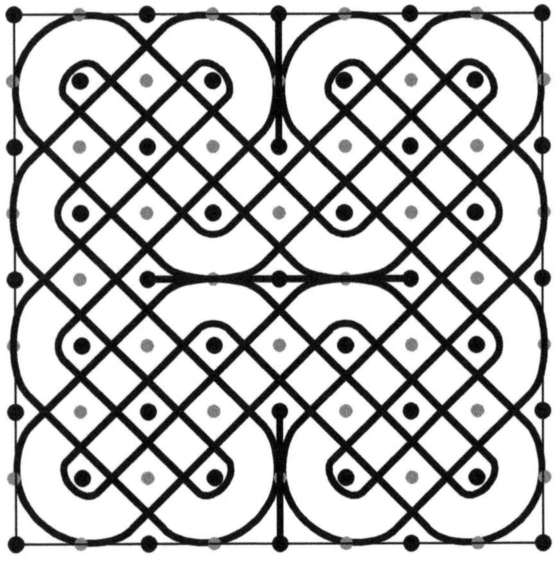

Next add corners on the knot to tie up all the remaining loose ends. Some patterns (depending on where you put your walls) may or may not have bends or corners to add. However, all the loose strands should have something to connect to. If there are loose strands that can't connect to anything, make sure to check that box corners are on big dots and that the walls you've added are going from big dot to big dot.

Modifying the Basic Knot...

Now begin to make the strands of the knot interweave. As before, each strand as it interweaves must go over and then under any other strand it intersects as you follow its path. To start over/unders, pick a point of intersection on the knot. It doesn't matter where. At this intersection, erase part of the strand to one of the ropes of knot, making the illusion of one strand passing over the other.

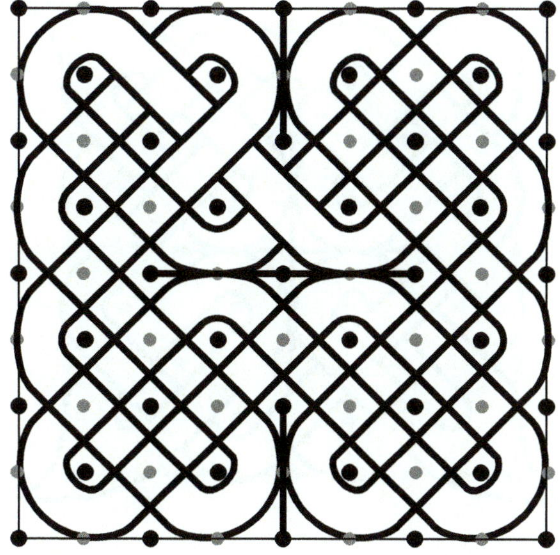

Continue to follow one strand of knot, erasing as you go, alternating whether it goes over or under the next strand it meets. Again, if you reach the end of the knot's path and there are still strands of over/under that haven't been erased, simply pick an unerased intersection and look at the other ones around it. If the strand leading into the intersection has just come from under another strand, erase your lines so the strand now passes over this one. Continue until all the intersections have been erased to complete the knot.

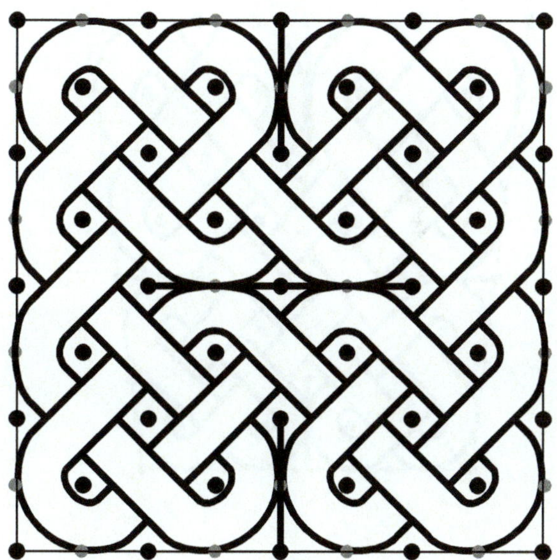

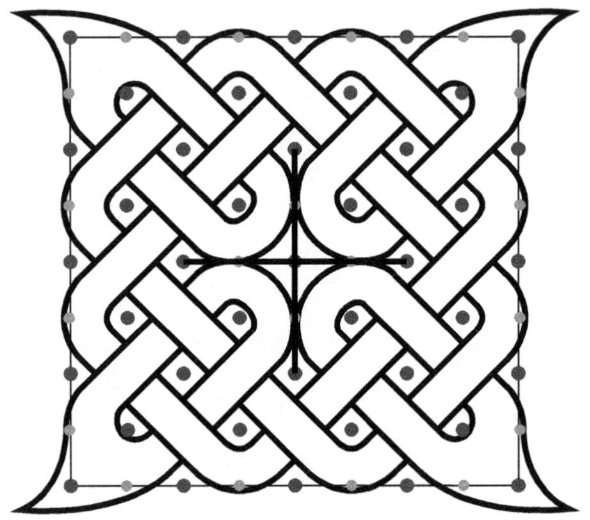

In this example I have used a different wall pattern and some fancier corners to give the knot some personality.

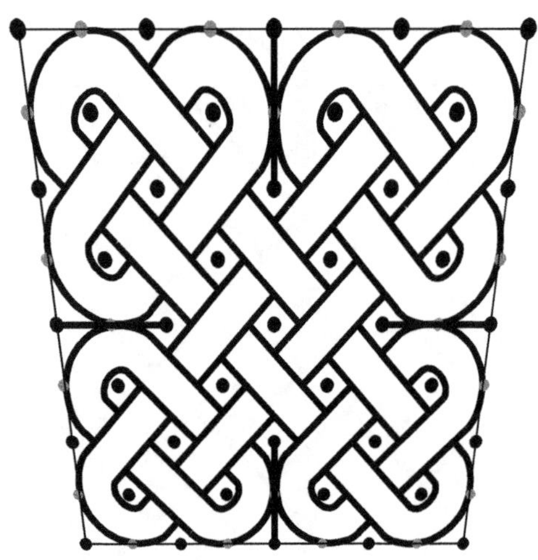

In this example a skewed dot pattern makes the upper knotwork appear bigger and thicker, while the lower portion is compressed and smaller. The techniques we used before are exactly the same; we've just changed the dimensions of the dot grid, which forces the knot to change to follow it. These changes to the dot grid are most easily done on a computer, but with patience they can be graphed out by hand as well.

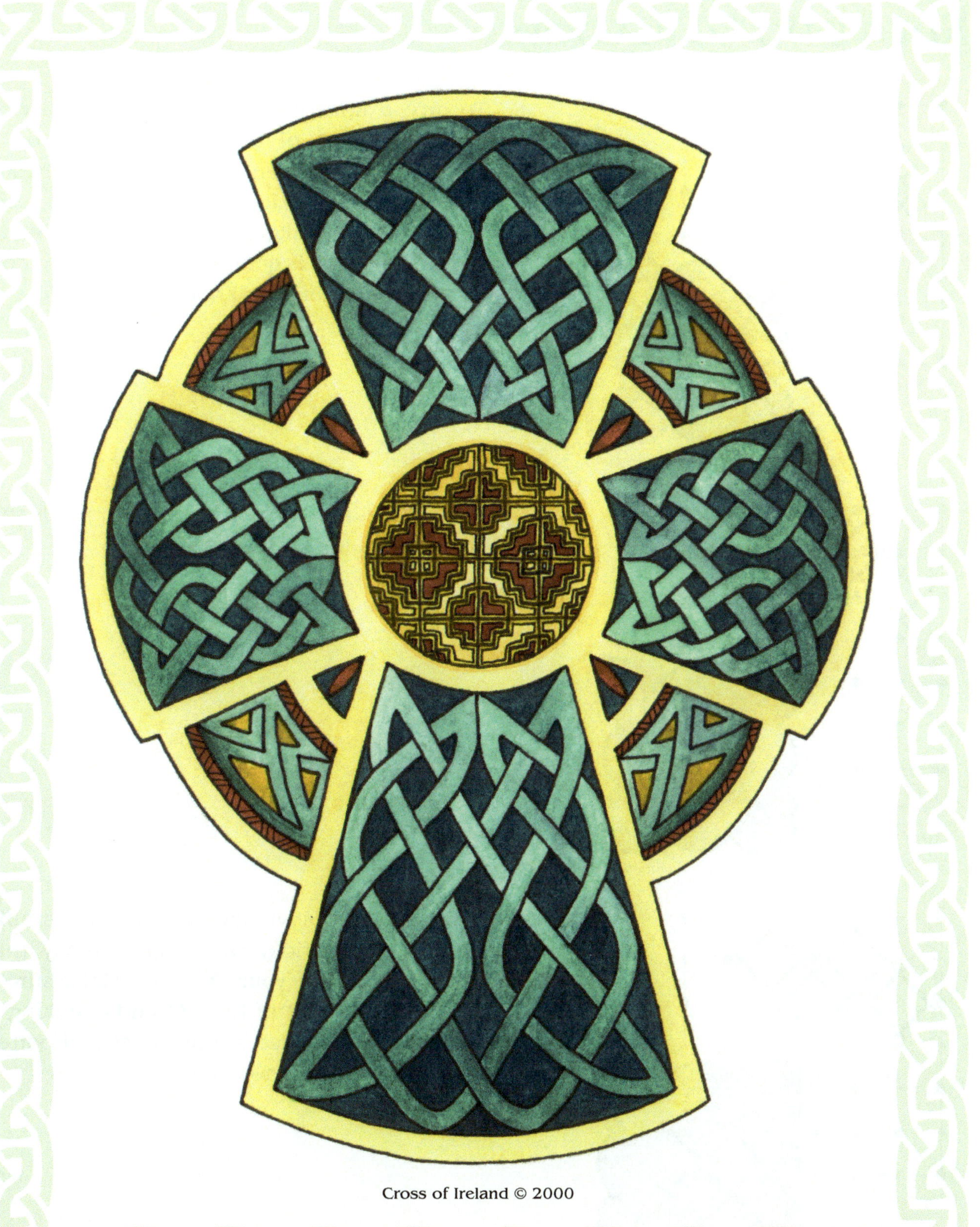

Cross of Ireland © 2000

Knotting Variations

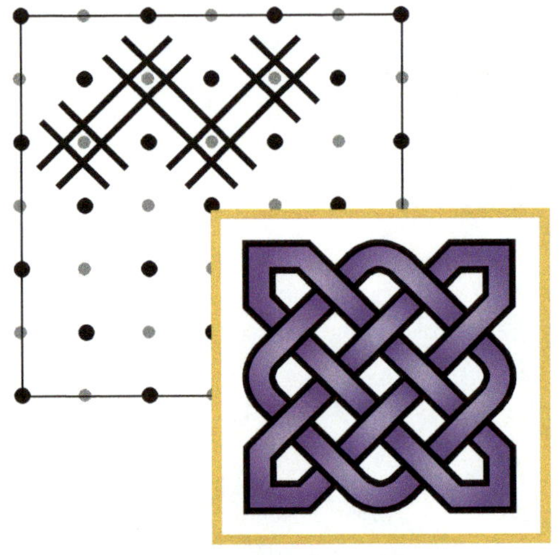

To give a knot personality, you can vary the overall thickness of the knotwork strands by making the "X" pattern thinner or wider. Making them close to the little dots will give you a thin knot with lots of background area showing behind the knot. This look is great when you want to color the background and the knot different colors.

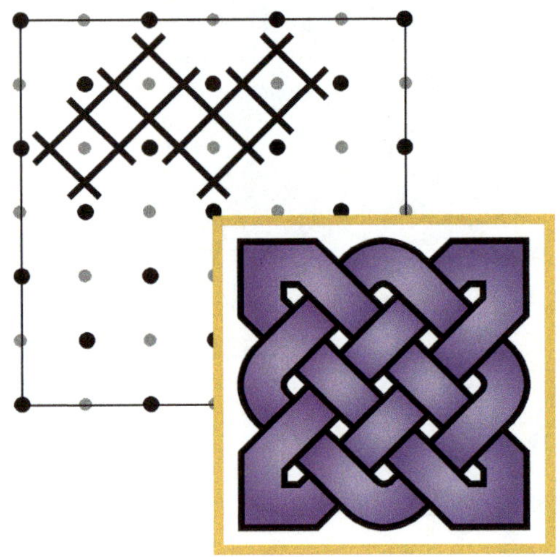

A medium-thick "X" pattern will produce a medium-thick knot after it's woven.

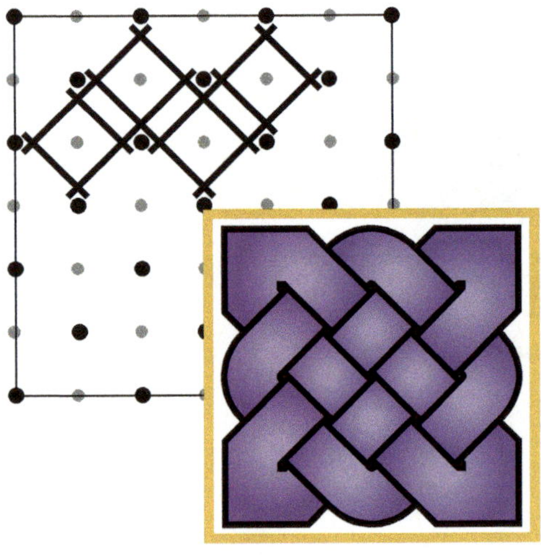

Super thick "X"s will give you a thick, chubby knot. It can be tricky when doing really thick knots to tell where your "X"s are. Make sure to leave just a little bit of the "X" ends peeking so you don't get confused about the strand pattern when you're ready to weave it.

Knotting Variations...

You can also change the look of your knot by changing the style of the corners. Choose all the same corner styles in one knot or mix and match. Some common styles of corners include rounded corners, which give a soft and casual feel to the knot.

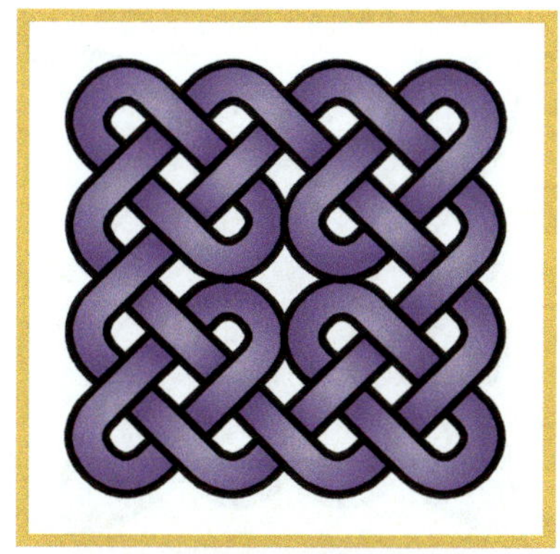

Squared-off corners offer a more precise or structured look to the knot.

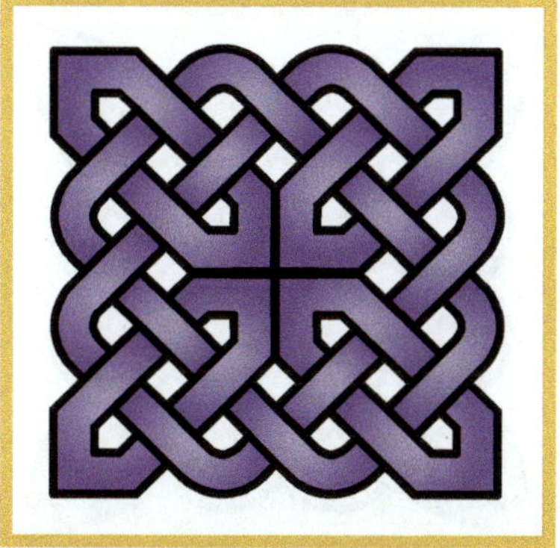

Mixed styles develop when you use one type of corner in some parts and then a different corner style elsewhere. This variation is great for large, complex knots because it adds more detail or interest to a larger piece.

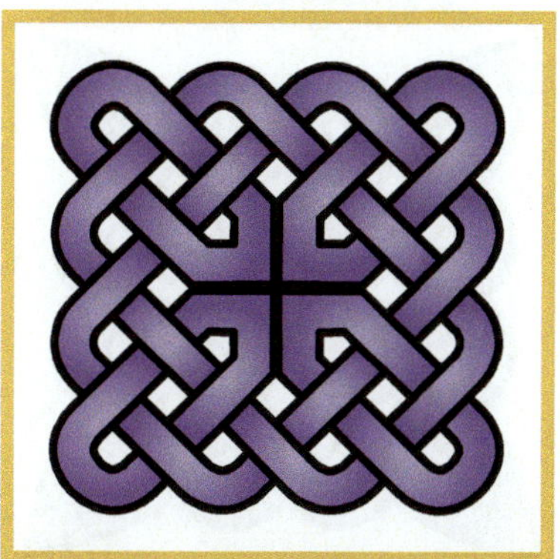

Elongated or tapered corners can be used to soften the overall design—this helps to break up the grid look and gives the knot a more freeform appearance.

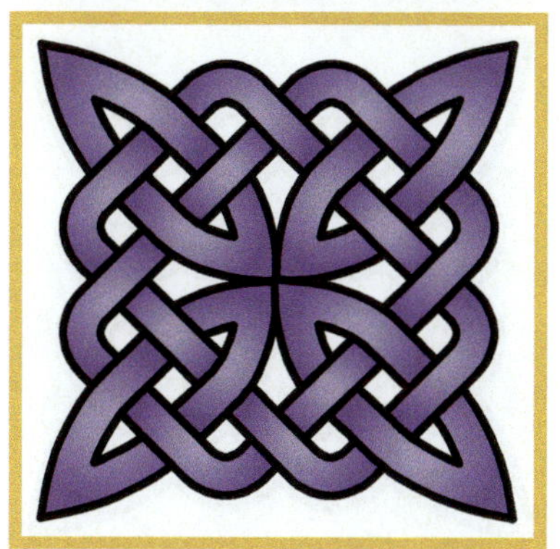

Knotting Variations...

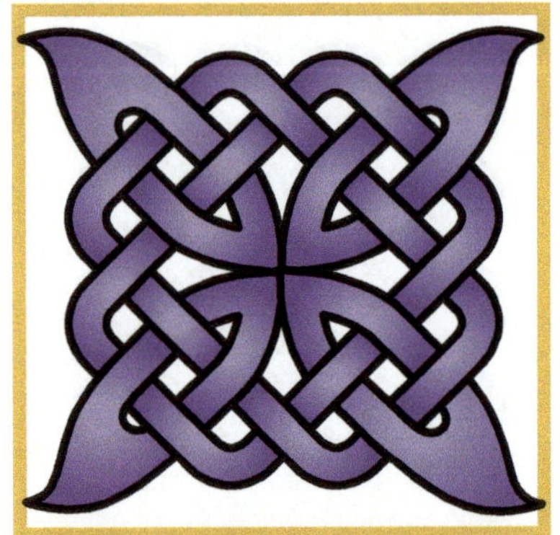

"Petal tips" is what I call a variation where each corner is pulled out and given a bit of a curve, mimicking a stylized flower petal or other shape.

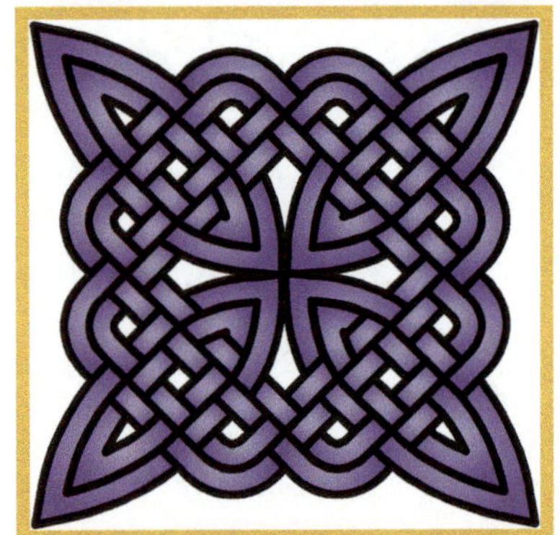

"Split weaving" is a technique where you add a center line to knotwork strands BEFORE you begin weaving. Once split, each narrow strand should be woven as its own continuous path. It adds an extra level of difficulty to the knot without having to create an entirely new design.

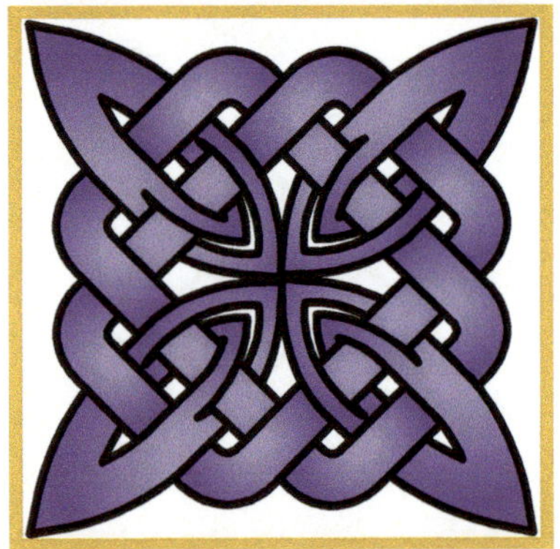

This is a variation on split weaving where instead of splitting the knot strand along the entire length of the path, you only split it for a small portion of the design.

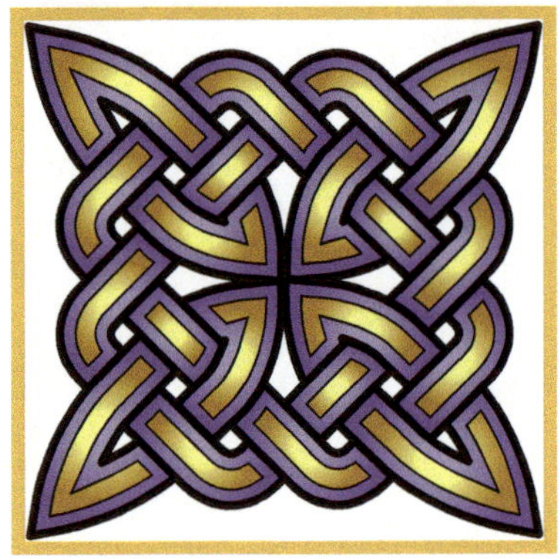

Inner outlines within finished knotwork strands can be added for an extra level of detail. This technique is easily mastered and is great for adding some extra color to your finished piece. Use a different shade as the main knotwork or a contrasting color for fun.

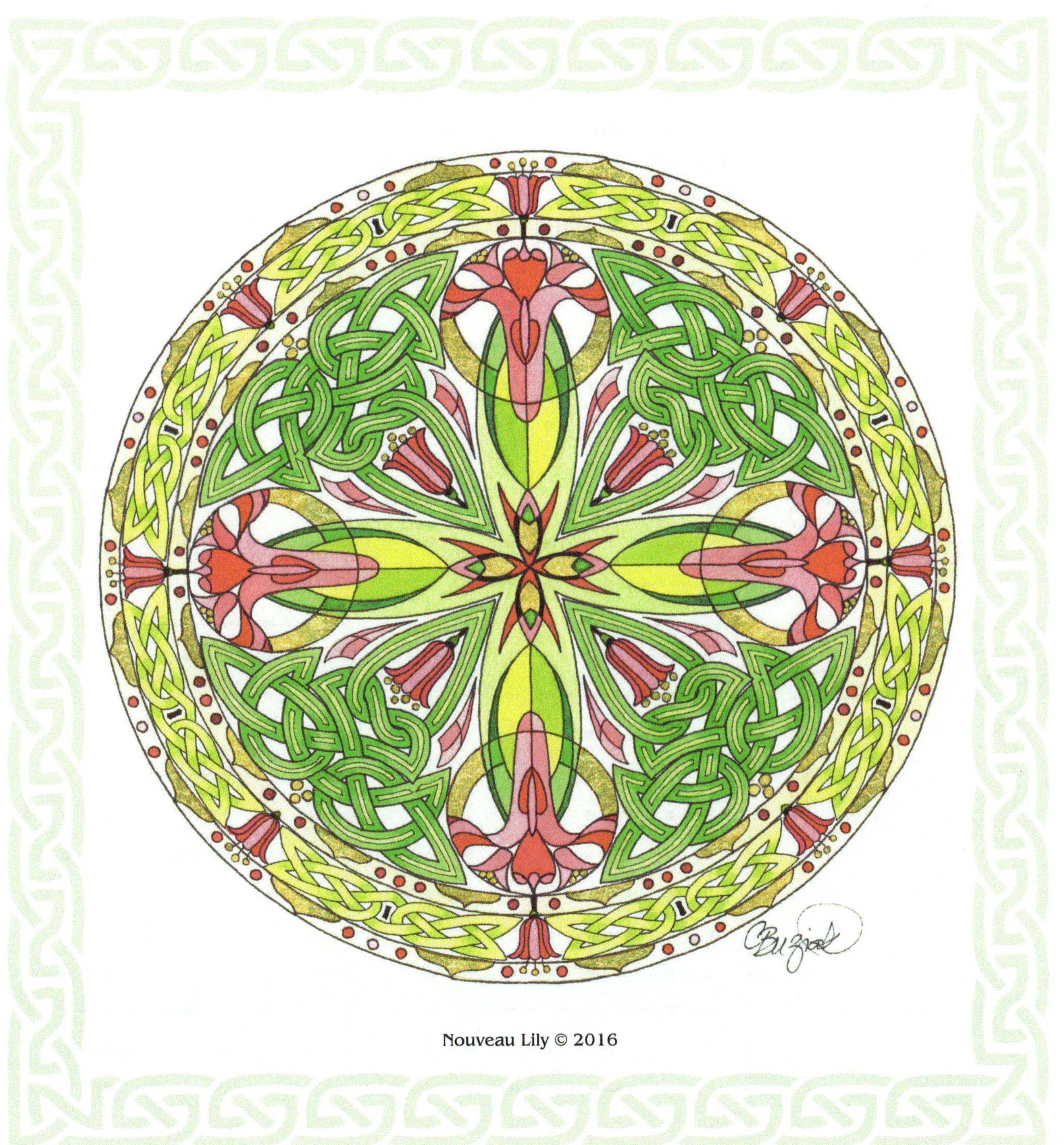

Nouveau Lily © 2016

Exercises

"Walls" can sprout from the edges of the box, occur in the middle of the box, or in any combination. Remember that they can only lie on the horizontal or vertical. There are two tricks in the exercises on this page. In one, there is a long continuation of the knotwork strand as it stretches around some walls to meet up with some other lines. In the other, there is a little "twist" or loop around a big dot, rather as if the knotwork strand is going around a fence post.

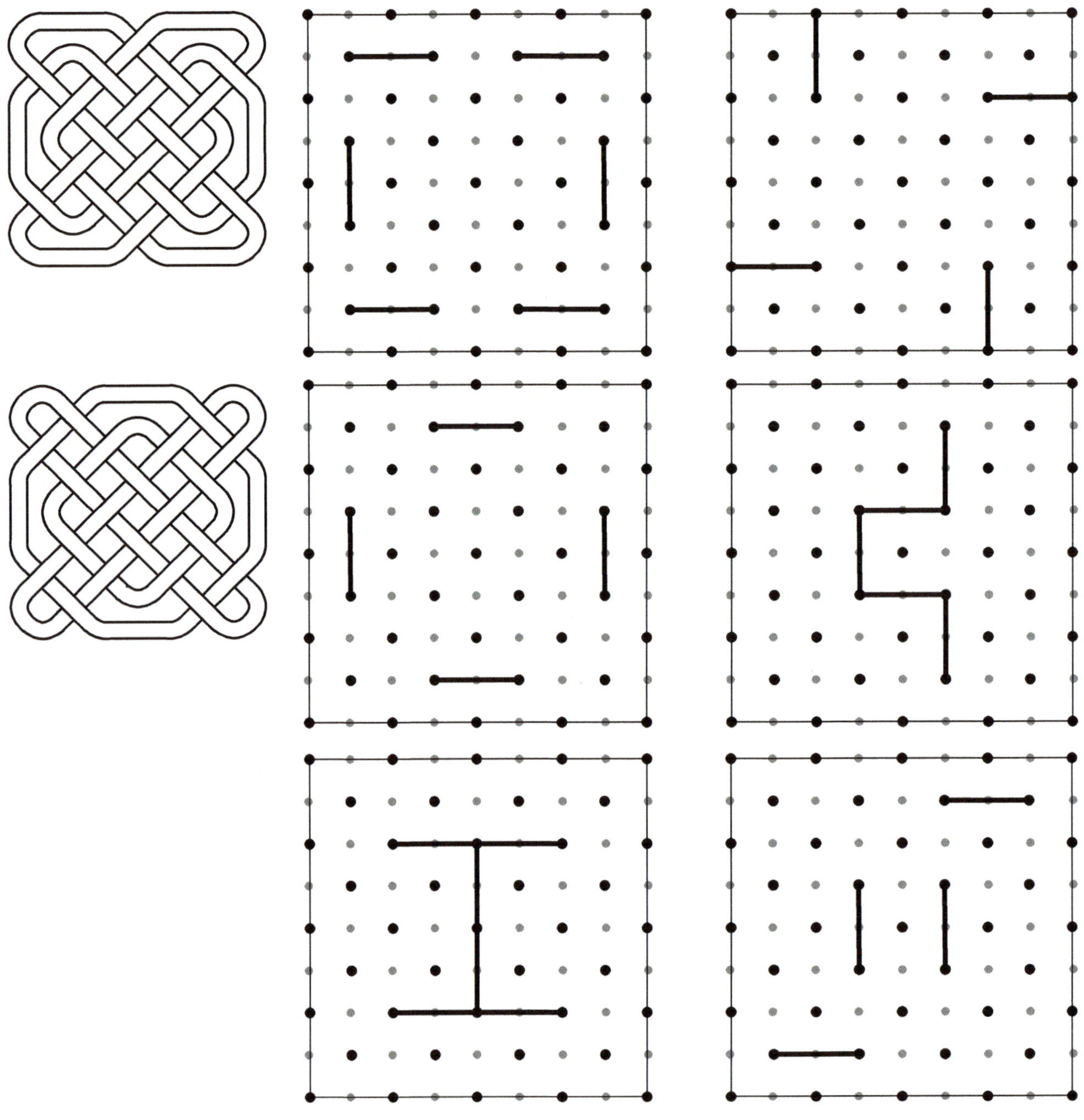

Here are examples of "walls" for some of the more common Celtic knots found in ancient manuscripts. In this exercise you'll see how deciding where to put your walls and how much space you leave between them can affect the look of your knot.

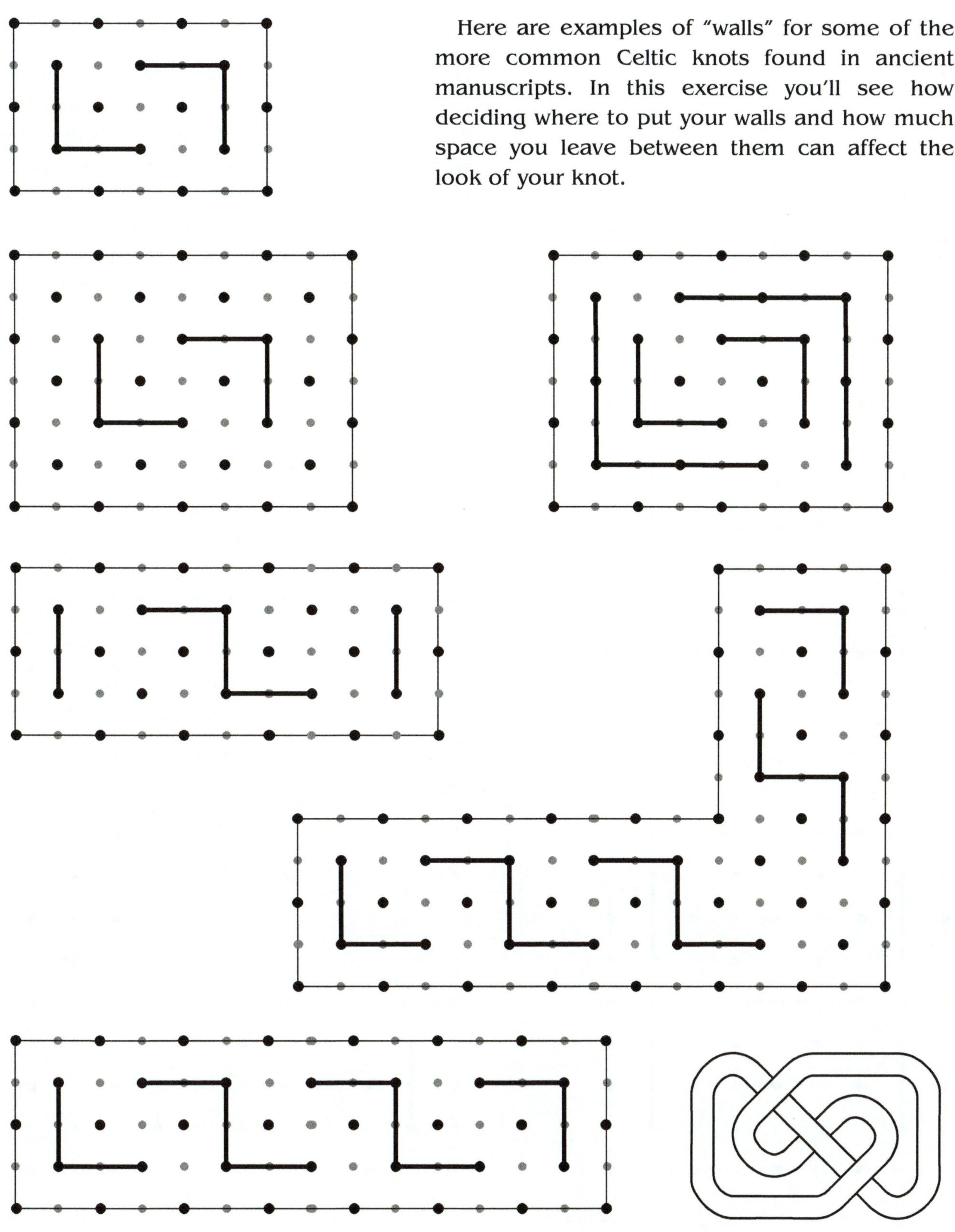

Exercises...

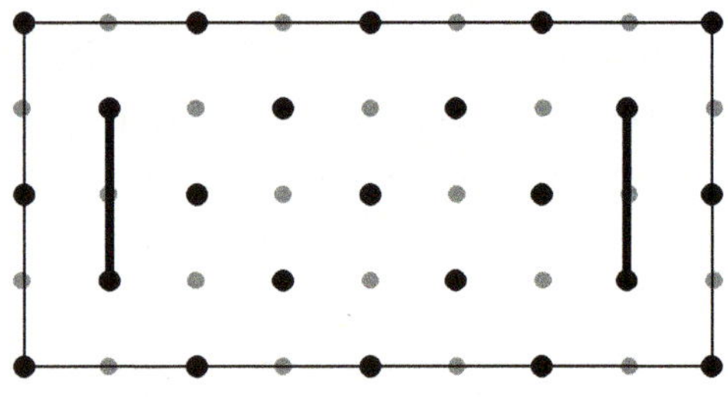

This knotwork example is sometimes called the Josephine's Knot. As the story goes, it resembles a common knot sailors used. Napoleon's Josephine was much loved by sailors so they named this knot after her. Some folks also call it a Lover's Knot because the two halves resemble two infinity symbols linked together. Neither name is historical in any way, but it makes a lovely knot pattern.

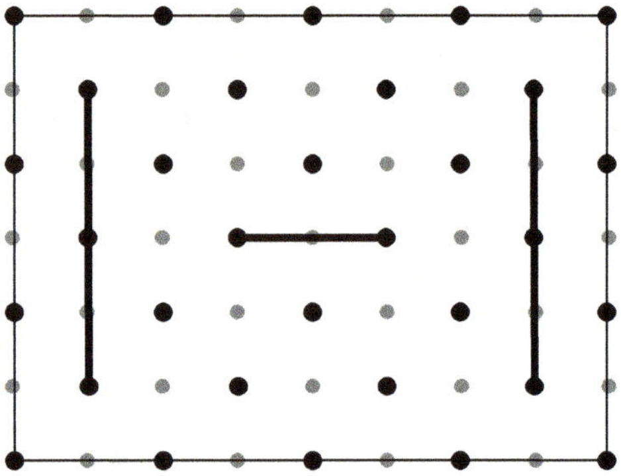

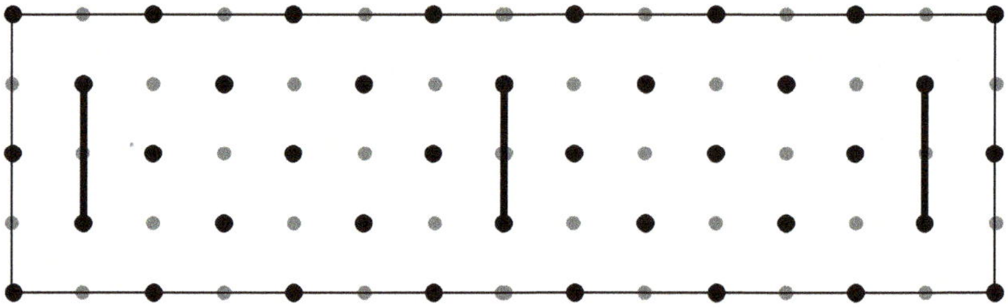

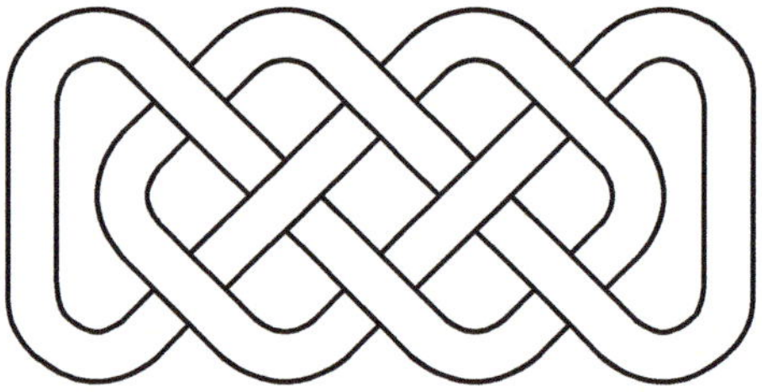

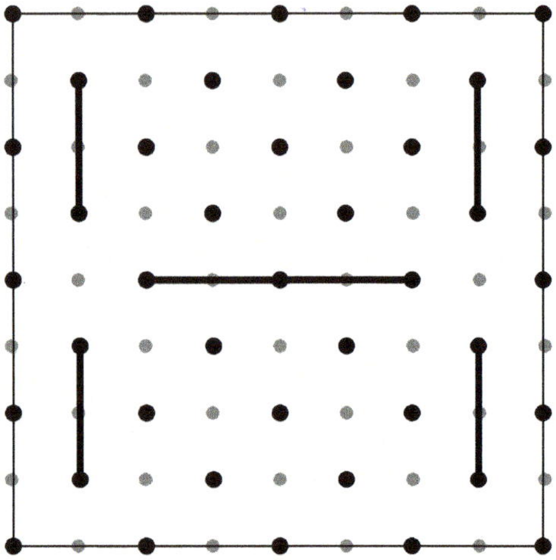

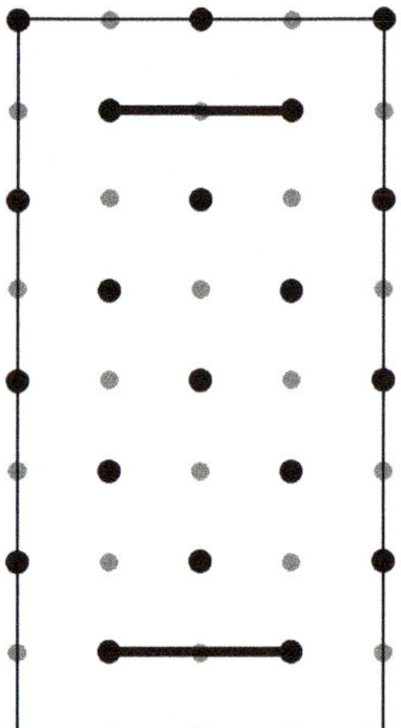

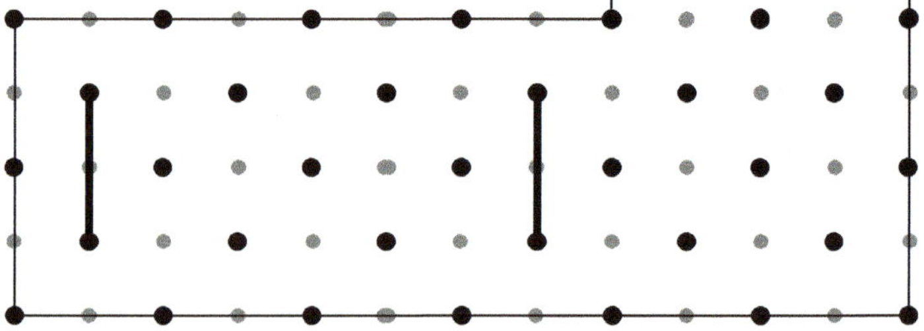

Exercises...

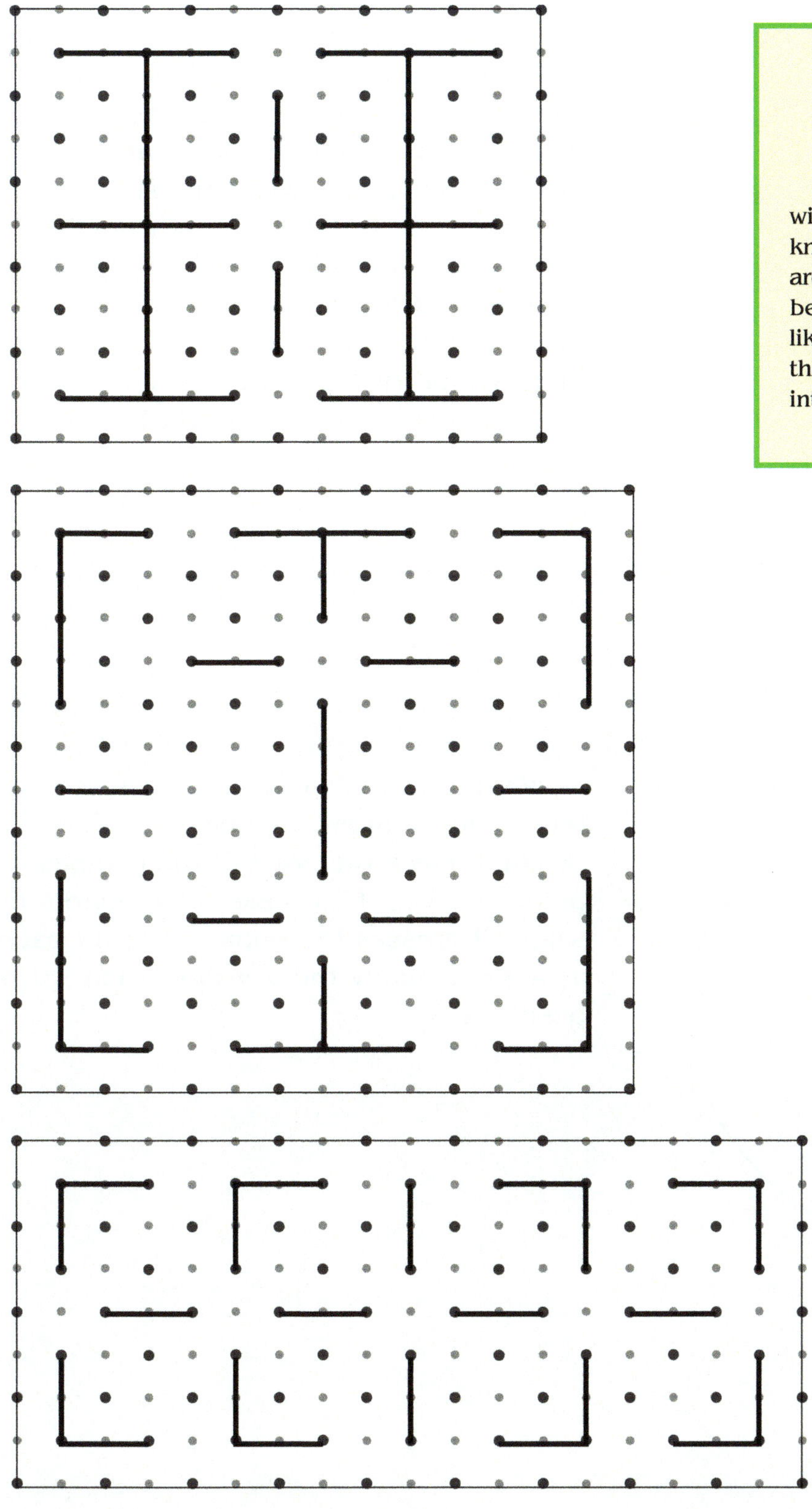

Tip

All the designs on this page will have a long strand of knotwork in the outer channels around the outside edge. Don't be afraid to have long strands like these in your work—they're what's going to make it interesting when it's finished.

The Trefoil Knot

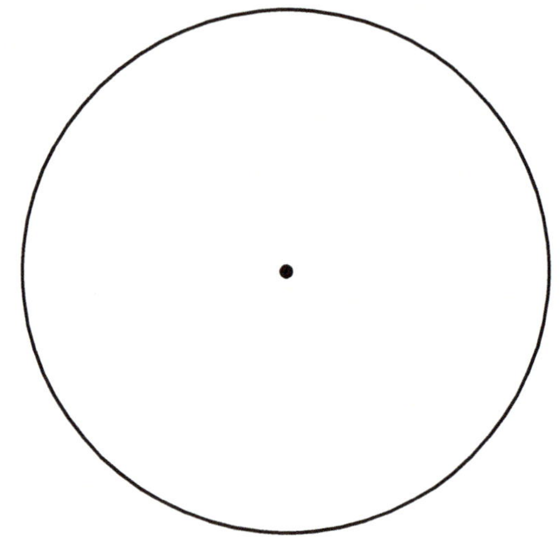

An important knot shape used in Celtic art is the Trefoil design. Also called the Trinity Knot, it's characterized by a triangular shape and has three main "lobes" of knotting to form the triangle. It can be made in many variations!

To make the Trefoil knot, you'll need a compass and a piece of regular paper. Set the compass to an average size and make a circle that is at least three inches in diameter on the page. Make sure there's a bit of room around the circle on your page, as the finished knot will be slightly larger than this initial circle.

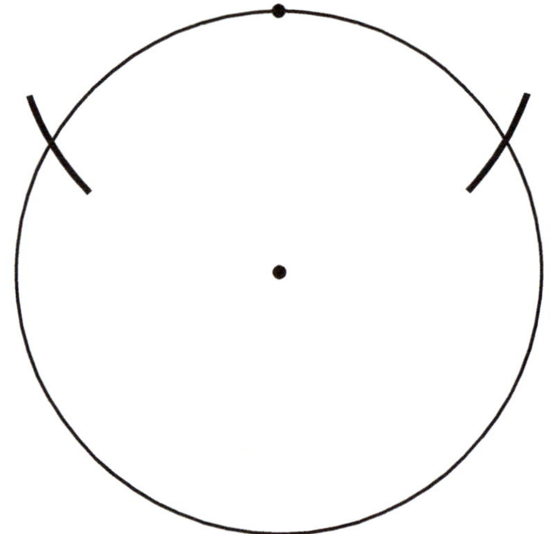

Without changing the compass setting, mark the circle at approximately the twelve o'clock position. Place the point of the compass on this point and use it to make small marks or ticks where it crosses the initial circle on each side, at approximately the 2 o'clock and 10 o'clock positions.

The Trefoil Knot...

Now place the compass on one of the marks you've just made—it doesn't matter which one you do first. Draw a semi-circle within the initial circle. It should start at the twelve o'clock point and end in the lower quarter of the circle. It's not necessary to make a whole circle, but the ends should extend a little past the outer edges of the original circle.

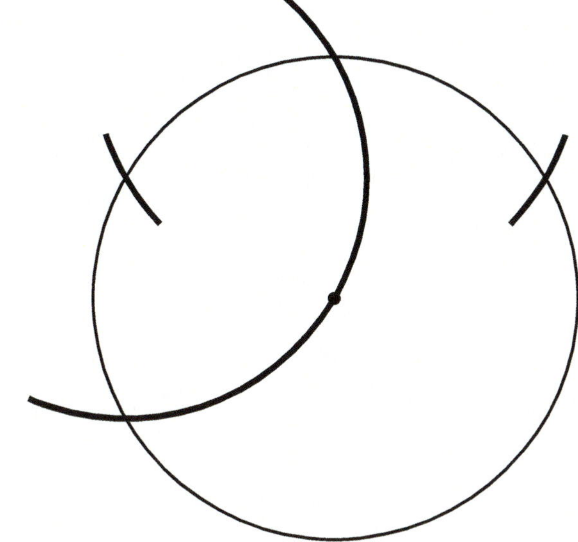

Make the other arc the same as you did the first one, but now from the opposite side. The two arcs should cross at the center point of the circle. If they don't, check to make sure the compass setting was not accidentally changed. It should still be the same size as the first circle.

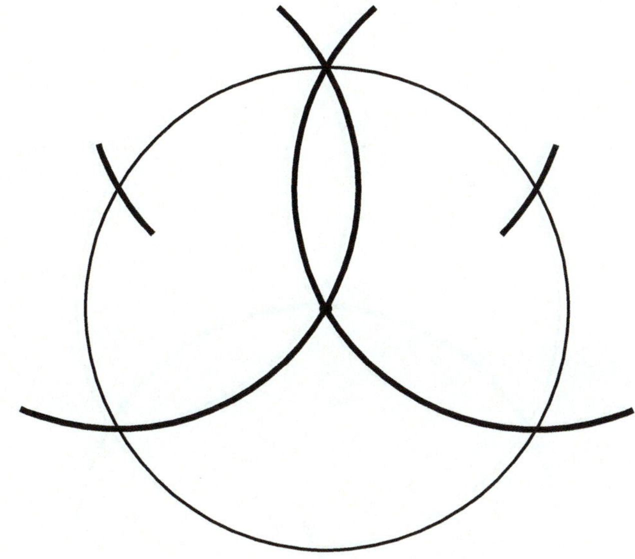

The Trefoil Knot...

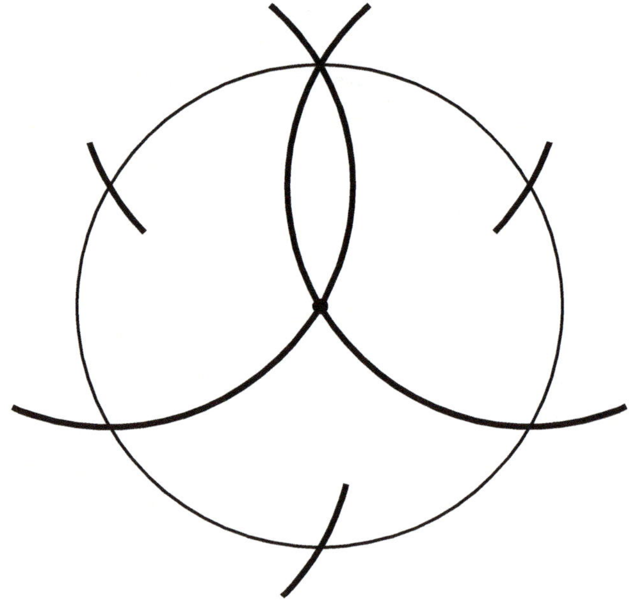

Now place your compass point on the spot where one of the arcs passes over the original circle and make another tick on the bottom of the circle. You don't need to make a mark on either side of the arc, just on the lower half at the 6 o'clock position.

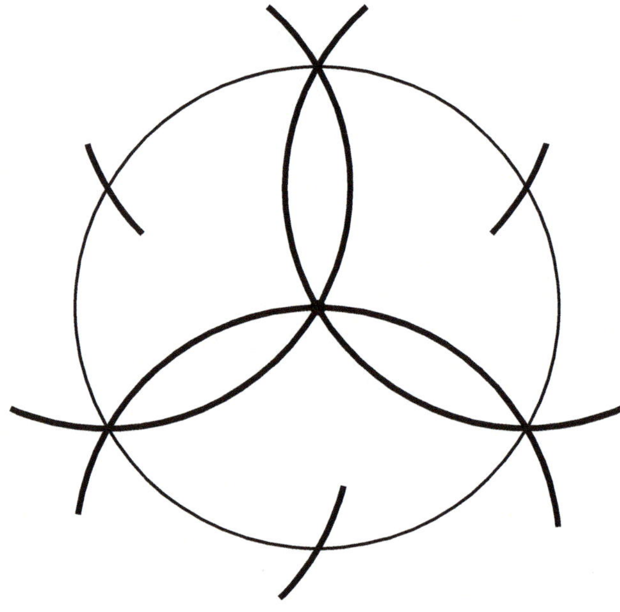

Place your compass on this bottom mark and draw another arc from side to side within the circle. This is the basic skeleton of the Trefoil Knot. All that's left to do is double up the lines and erase the overs and unders.

The Trefoil Knot...

Using the measuring scale on your compass, enlarge its diameter now by however much you want the thickness of the knotwork strands to be. Place the compass point back onto the 10 o'clock, 2 o'clock, and 6 o'clock positions and draw a new arc from each position.

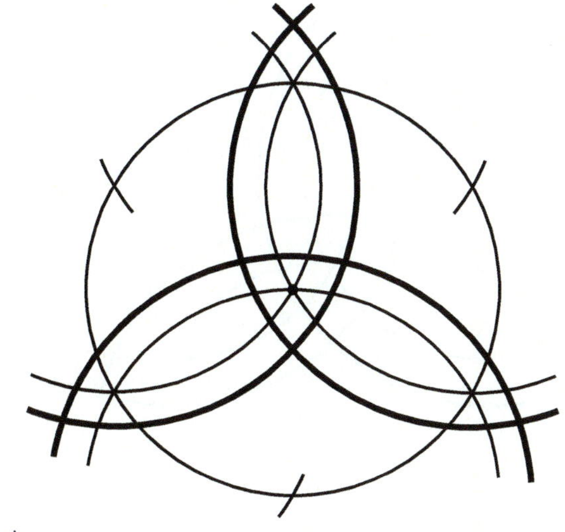

Once the circles and ticks are removed, you can see the shape of the Trefoil Knot beginning to take form. Clean up the corners of the knot so they come to nice points.

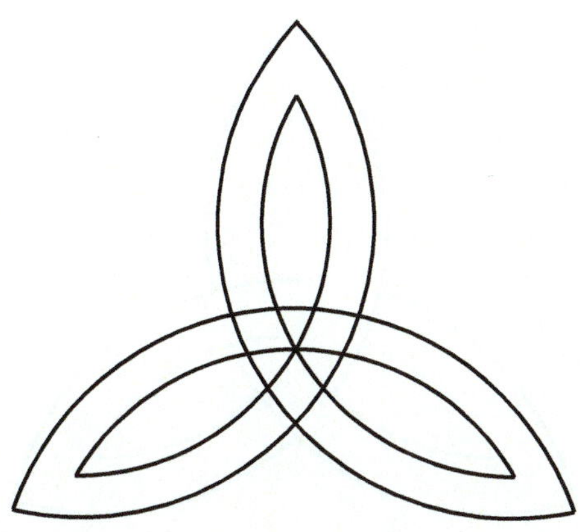

The Trefoil Knot...

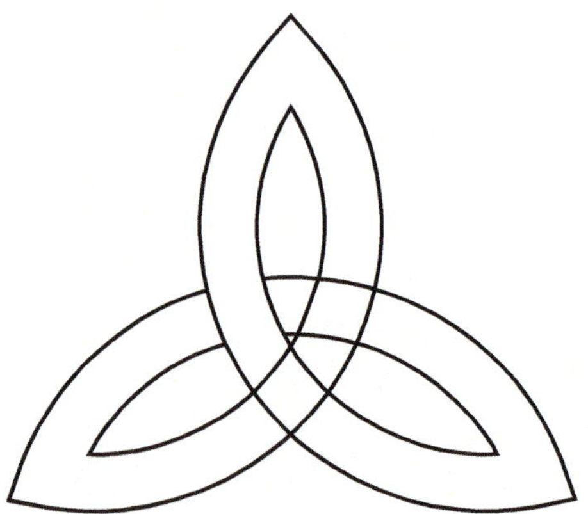

Pick a point where one of the knot strips intersects another and make it pass over the other, erasing the under lines from the "under" strip from within the "over" strip.

Following the same strand around, the next intersection should be the opposite of the first (so if it was an under, this will be an over), and the final intersection will be the same as the first, finishing the knot.

The Trefoil Knot...

This variation was created by making the original arcs larger so they extended past the centerpoint of the original circle, rather than passing through the center. It produces a looser, more open-looking knot.

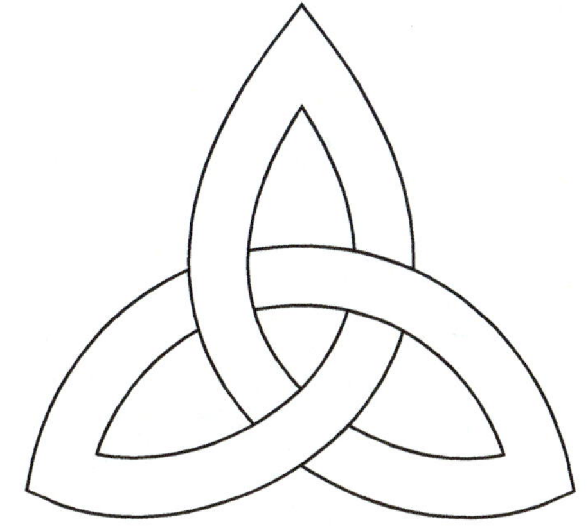

With the extra space in the knot above, I can add designs such as circles, hearts, or triangles to give me more things to weave through and increase the complexity of the knot.

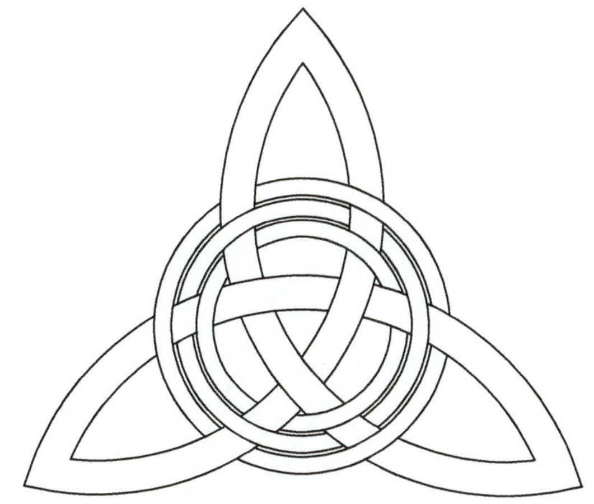

If the second set of arcs are a good deal larger than my original ones the result is a big, chubby trefoil.

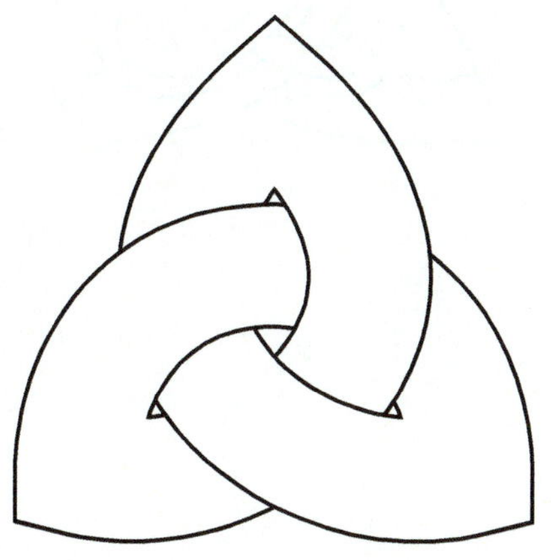

The Trefoil Knot...

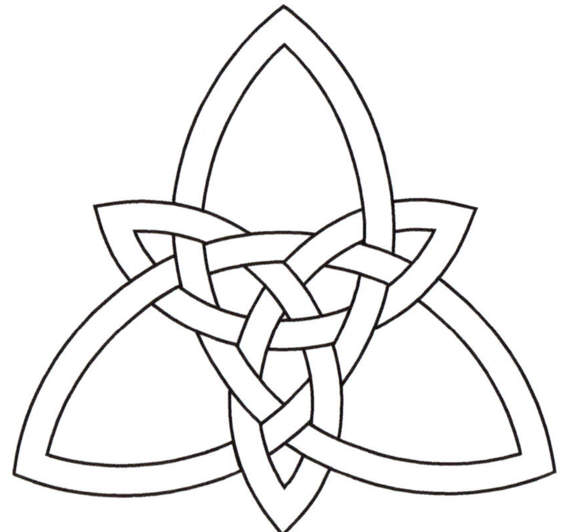

For this example, I made my original knot quite open and loose and then created a smaller, tighter knot. The smaller knot is placed at 60 degrees of the first, so it appears rotated within the first.

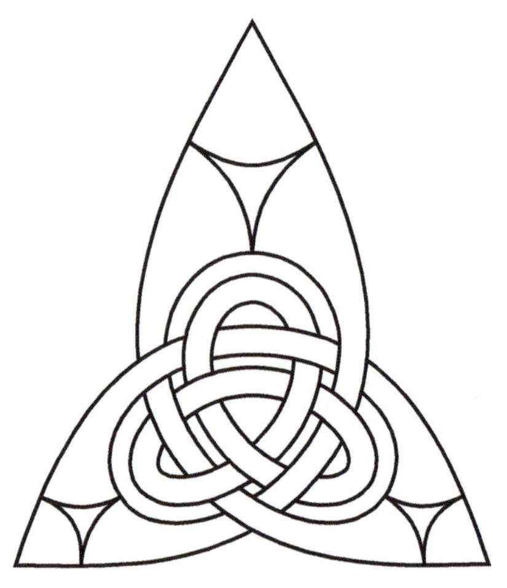

In this variation the original knot is loose but a second smaller one has been set within it without being turned. Notice how the differing shape of the corners of the inner knot make it more interesting than merely a bunch of repeating corners.

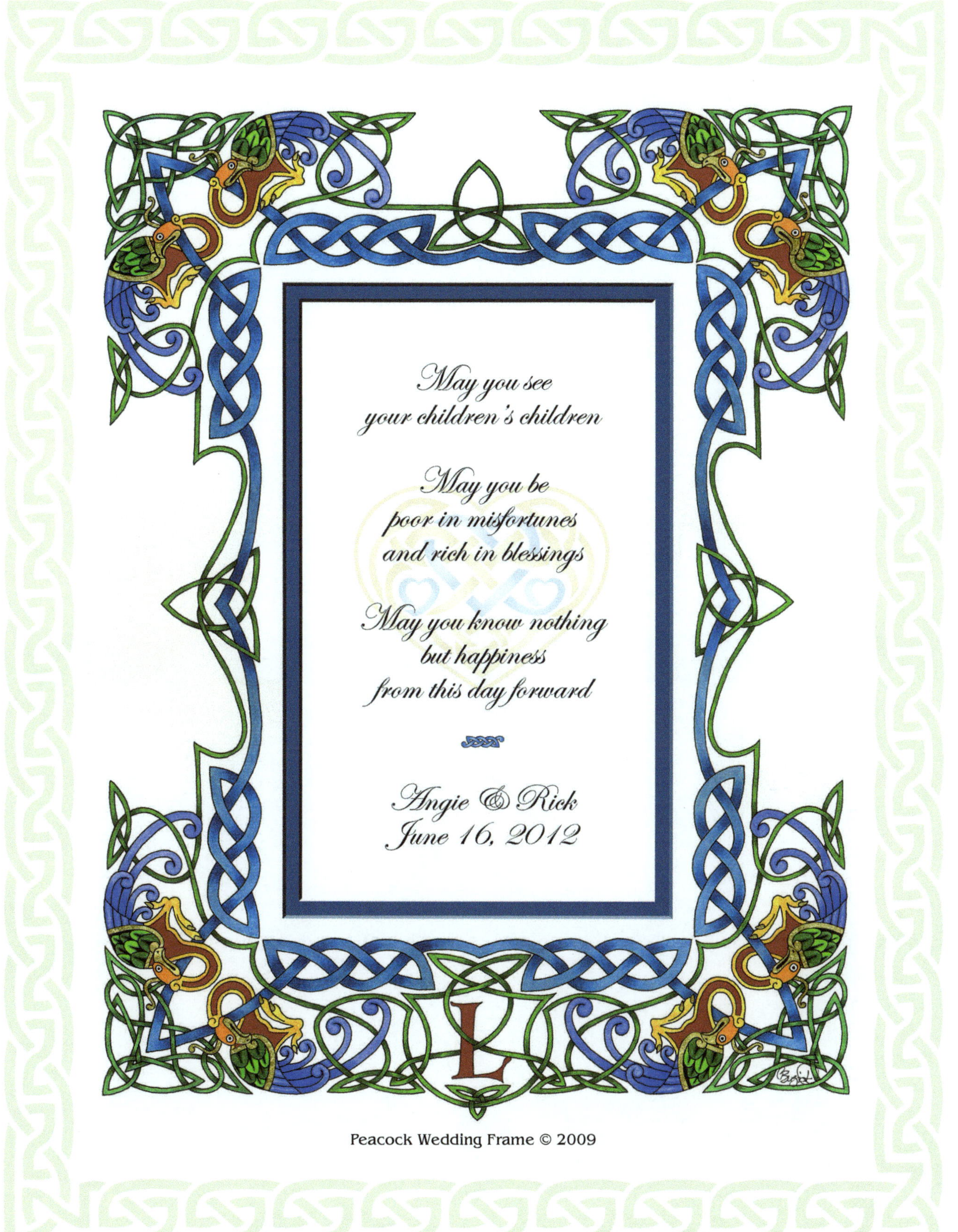

Peacock Wedding Frame © 2009

BORDERS & CORNERS

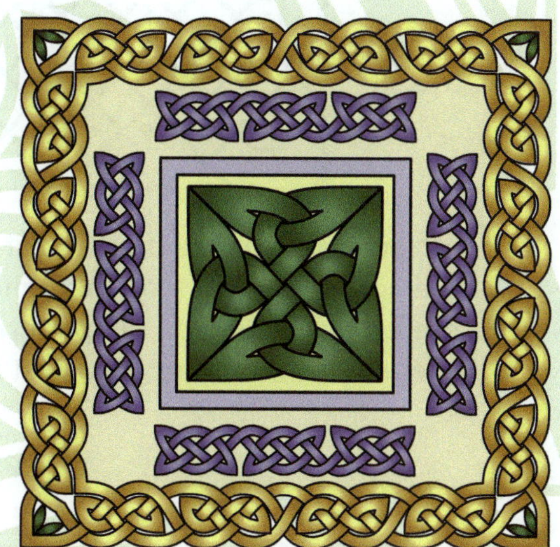

Borders

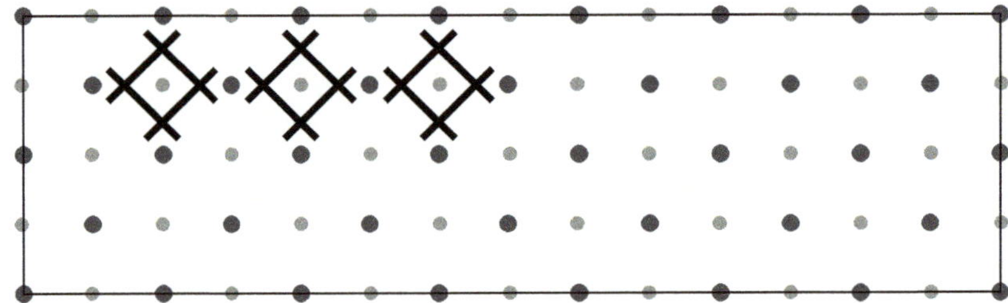

To make a Basic Knot Border, mark off a section on the dot paper that is at least three big dots high. The width, between big dots, is up to you. Remember to put the corners of the border on BIG dots only. Cover every little dot within this marked-off area with a double lined "X."

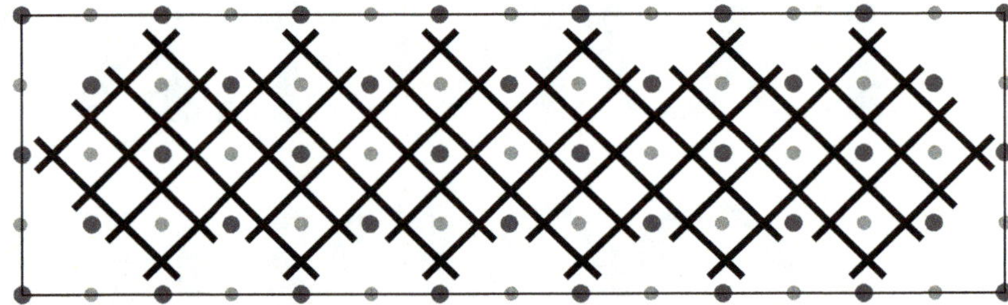

Continue until the marked-off area looks much like this. All of the little dots will be crossed over with the double "X," which will create a grid-like structure. The basic knot border is really a basic knot that extends out over a larger area, so instead of being square, it's rectangular. All the same rules and processes apply as before.

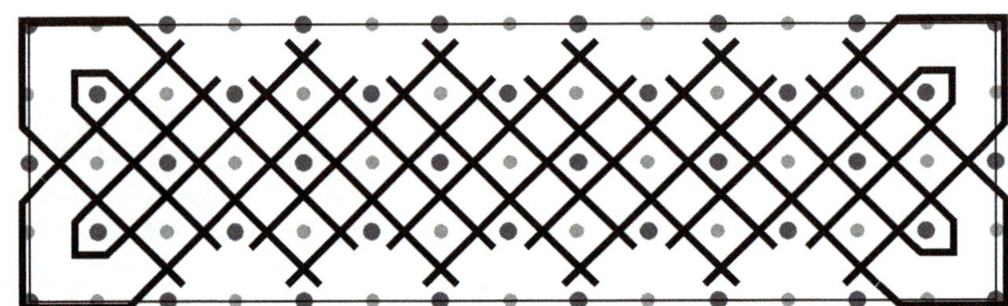

Now start to close the ends of all of the knot lines. Connect the lines in all the corners, or work on the bends on the horizontal and vertical first, if you prefer. Depending on the pattern, the corners or the bends can be easier to see, so do whichever is easiest for you.

Borders...

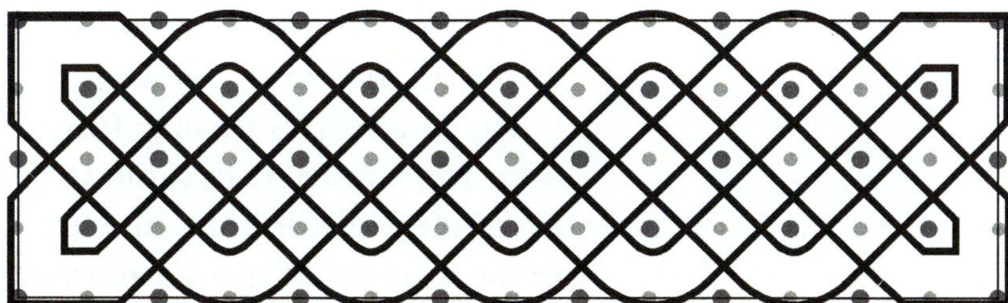

Now add all the bends along the horizontal and vertical so that all the knot line ends are used. There shouldn't be any leftover ends. Note that this example is a narrow border so it has no bends on the vertical to connect.

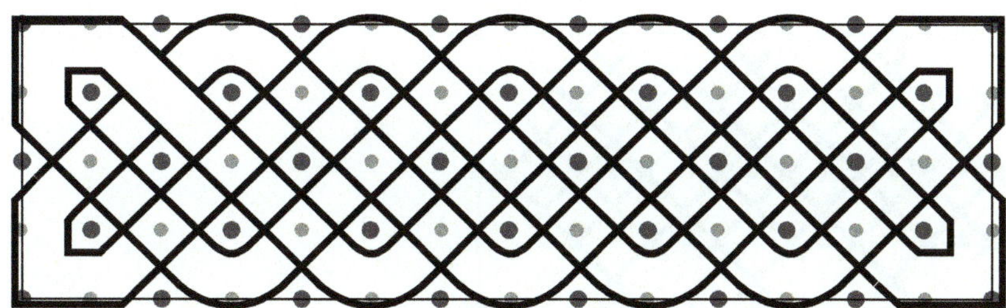

Now begin to weave the overs and unders. Pick an intersection and erase the center so that it appears as though one knot strand is passing over the other. Follow that strand around, erasing so that it passes over and then under the next strand it meets. As you continue, you'll see a pattern to your erasing which is helpful when creating larger knots. Anything that falls directly in line (horizontally or vertically) with an "over" will also be an "over," or an "under" if it's an "under." This will also be helpful for double checking that the overs/unders have been erased correctly. In addition, it speeds up the erasing process when there are a lot of intersections to erase.

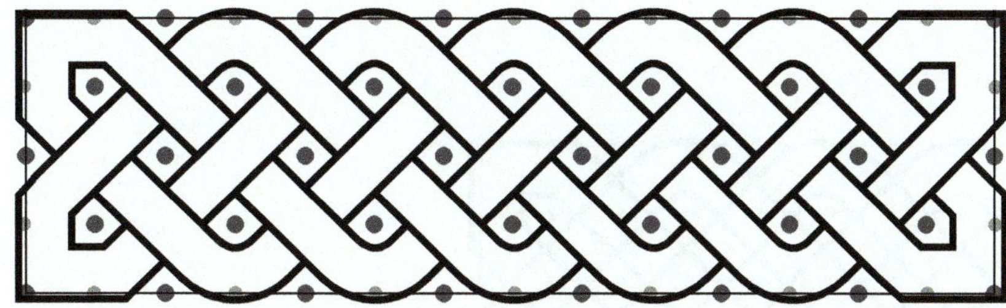

Here we see that our knot border has all been erased so that the overs/unders appear. You can now see how, if you look straight across the intersections on the horizontal or vertical, it's either all unders or all overs.

Corners

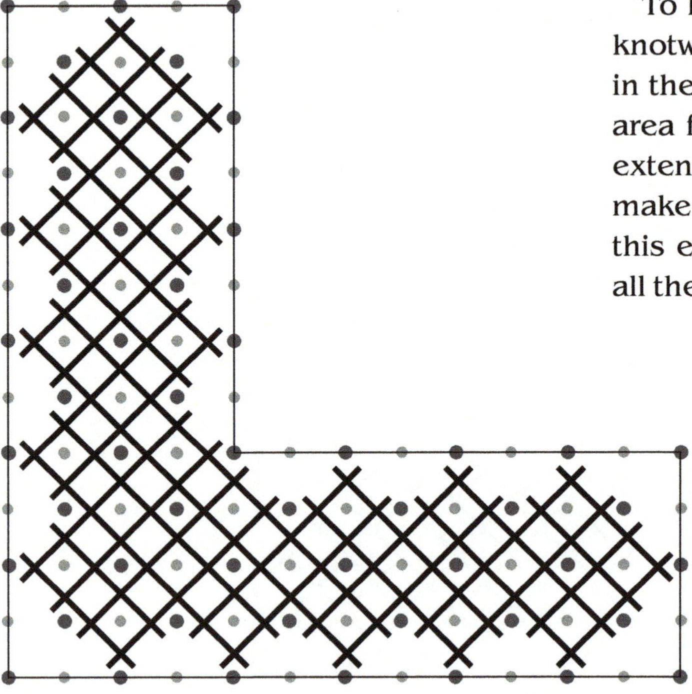

To knot around a corner or make a continuous knotwork frame or border, first mark off the area in the shape you desire. Here I've marked off my area for a corner, making it 3 big dots wide and extending around in an "L" shape. As always, make sure all of the corners end on a BIG dot. In this example I have crossed an "X" pattern over all the little dots that fall within my boundary box.

Add the bends on the horizontals and verticals, and the corners to the corners, until all the lines are connected.

Corners...

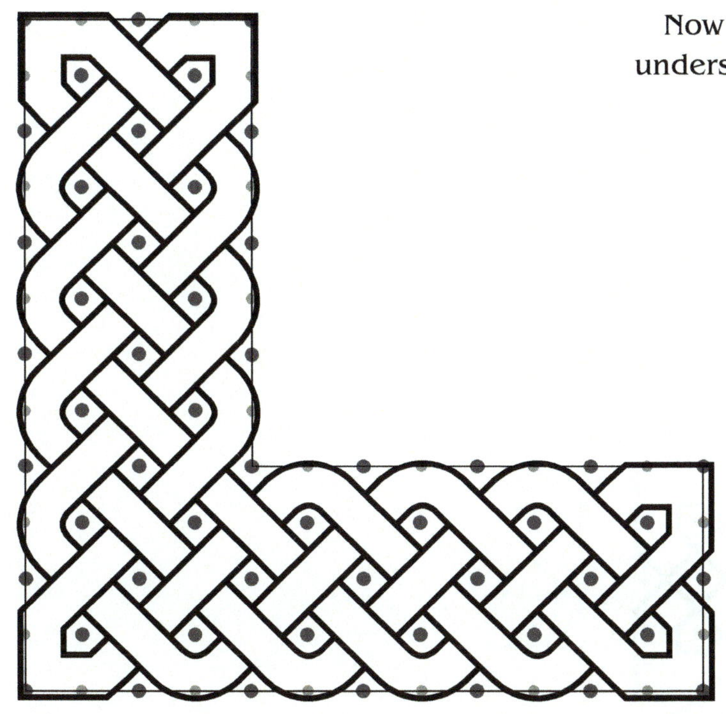

Now go through and erase all the overs and unders at all the intersections.

You can also make a more interesting corner for the border by making the knot poke out at the inner corner, like a notch. Any irregular shape can be made, as long as you make sure that the corners of the boundary box always fall on a BIG dot. As always, cross an "X" pattern over all the little dots that fall within the marked-off area.

Corners...

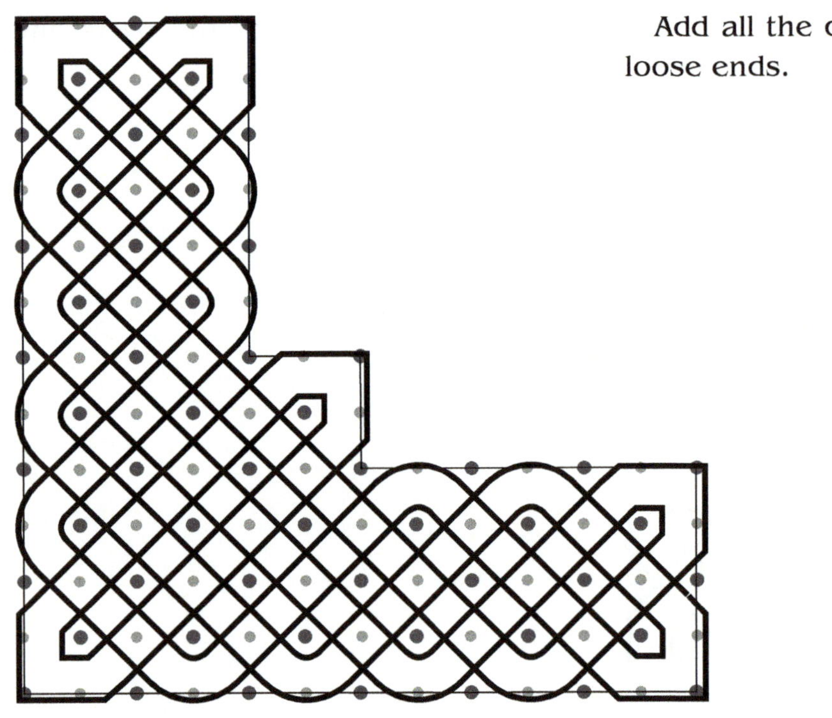

Add all the corners and bends to connect the loose ends.

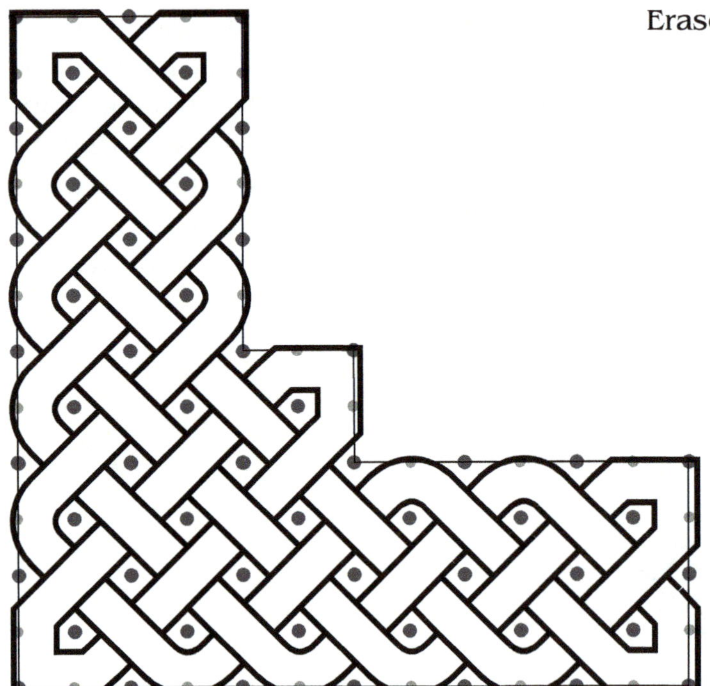

Erase your overs and unders, as usual.

Corners...

Using this technique it's possible to design any number of shapes. Simply mark off the boundary shape, add walls, and weave them up.

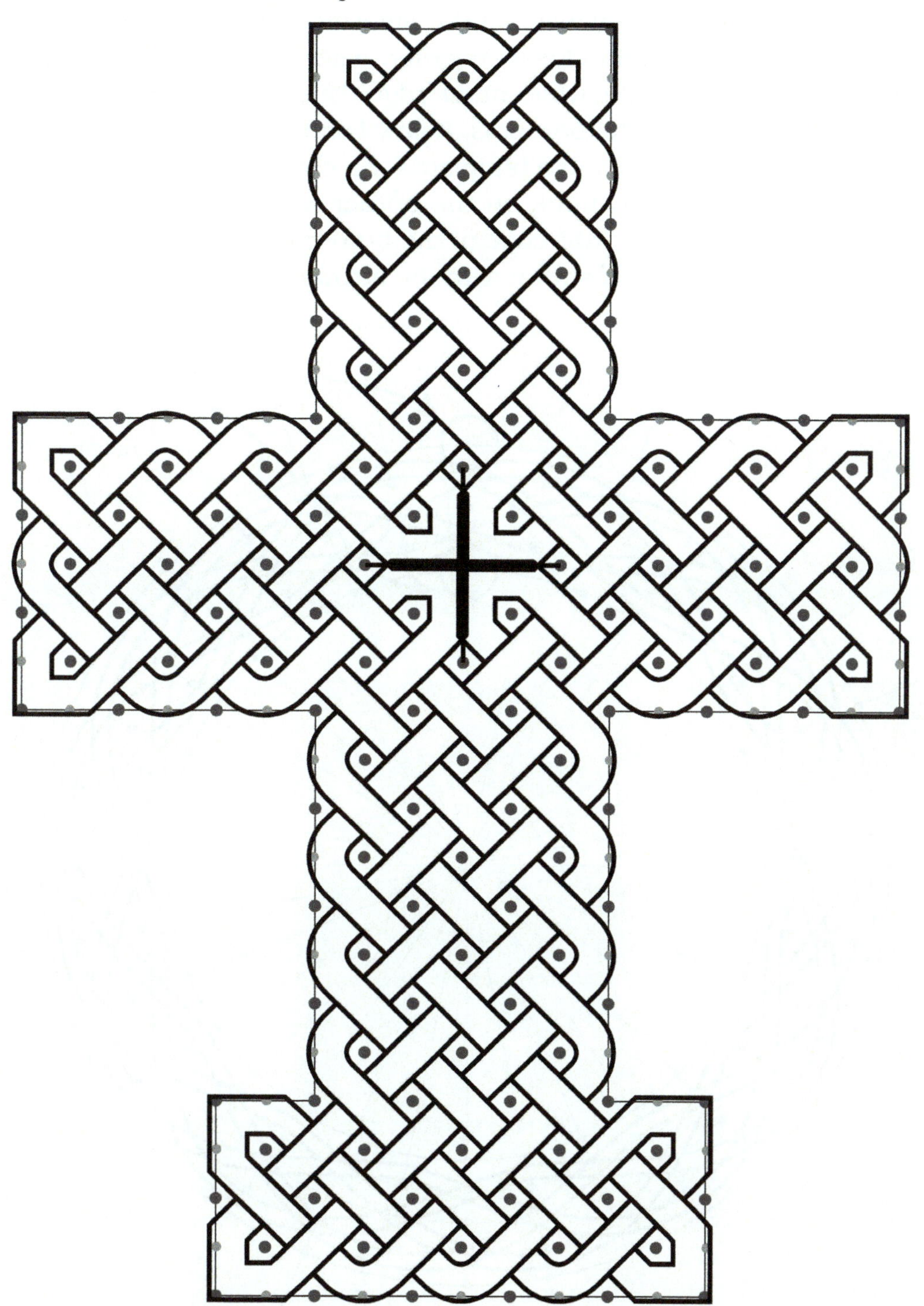

Knotting in a Ring

I am often asked how to knot a border in a circular shape so it makes a ring. The theory behind it is much like we have already practiced with our straight borders, except the border is curved around into a circular shape. The biggest difference is that the innermost dots you weave around are more compressed and closer together, whereas the outside dots are spread out as they span the wider outer edge. This effect will become more pronounced the thicker the border is. Below I show how a "3 Big Dot" wide border would go. You can find a template for a complete ring border at the back of this book. Simply mark off the border width desired, taking care that a big dot on the OUTSIDE edge of the border must coincide with a big dot on the INSIDE edge, as shown with the arrows below.

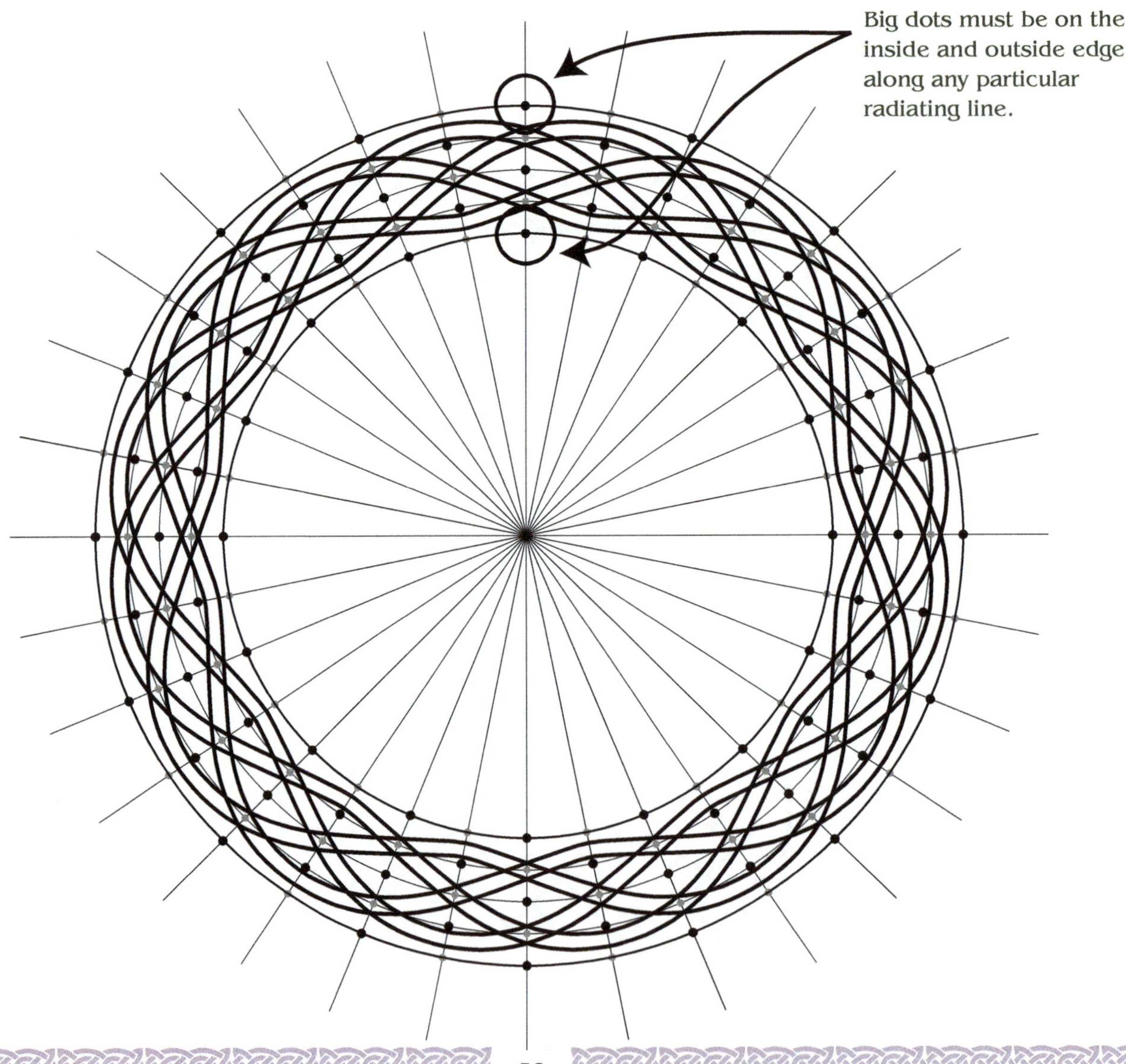

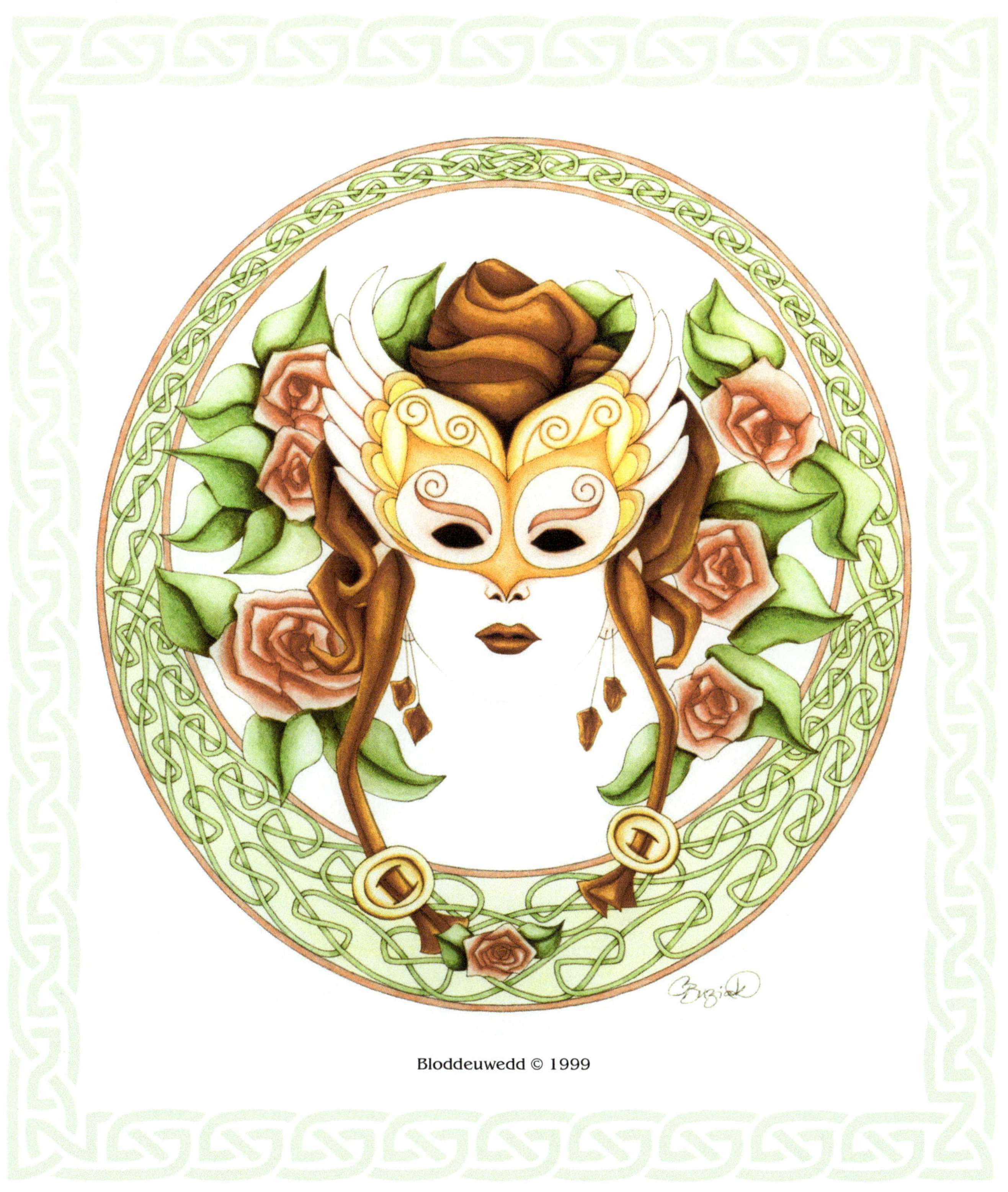

Bloddeuwedd © 1999

CROSSES

The Celtic Cross

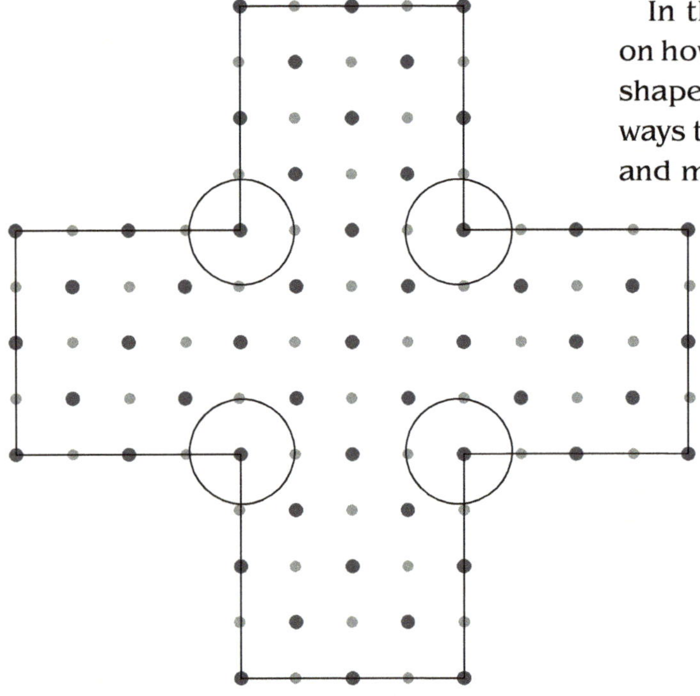

In the beginning knotwork chapter we worked on how to make knots in a wide variety of different shapes, including crosses. Now let's look at some ways to make variations on the basic cross shape and make it a little more traditionally Celtic.

Mark off a cross shape about 3 big dots x 3 big dots for each "arm" of the cross and add four circles to the "armpits" of the arms. These circles should be big enough to pass through some little dots inside the cross.

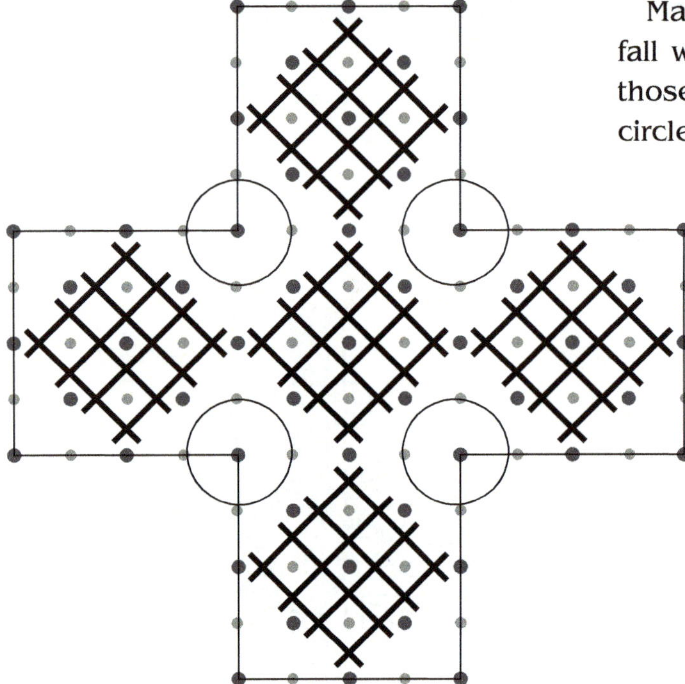

Mark the "X" pattern over all the little dots that fall within the cross but make sure not to reach those that fall on or within the little circles. The little circles should be treated like walls, essentially.

The Celtic Cross...

Add the corners and horizontal/vertical bends, as usual. Notice that in my example there are two unjoined ends of knot strands, pointing toward the little circles near each armpit. There are a few different options to join these up to something.

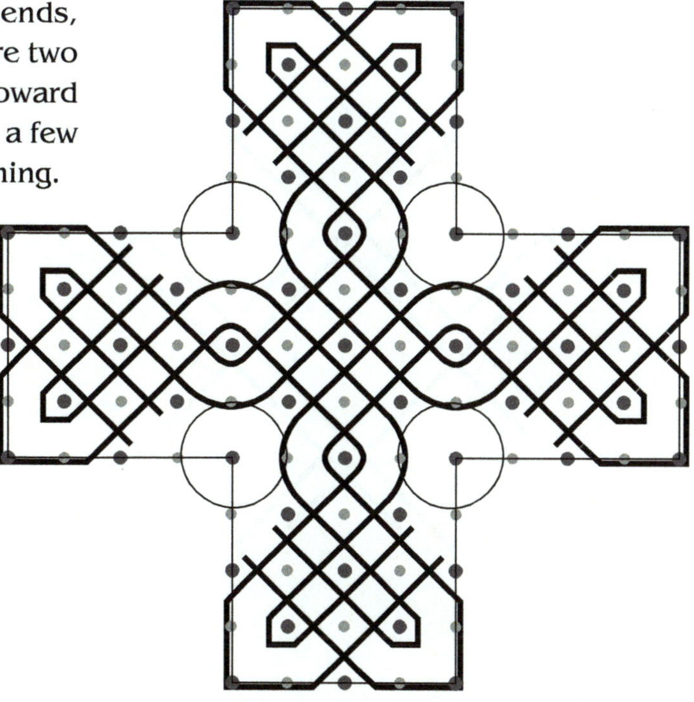

The simplest solution would be to just extend the loose strands outward, arcing them over the little circles and joining them to each other.

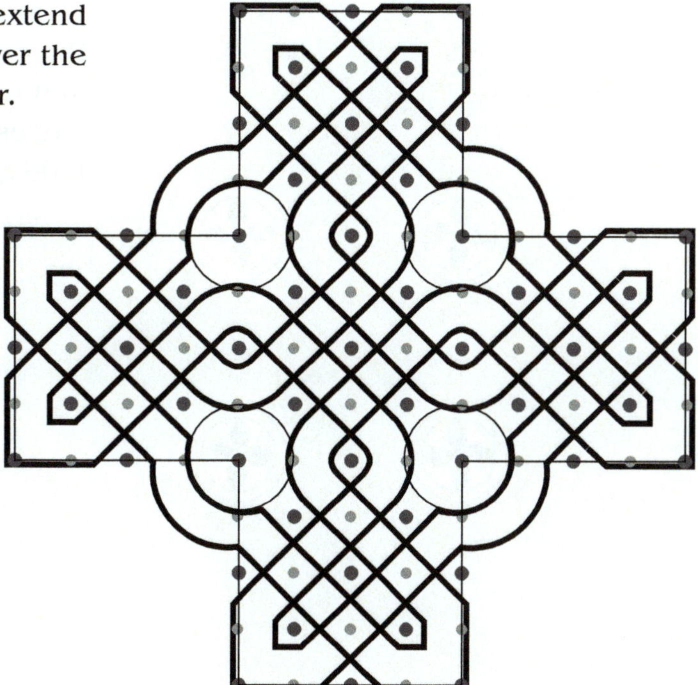

The Celtic Cross...

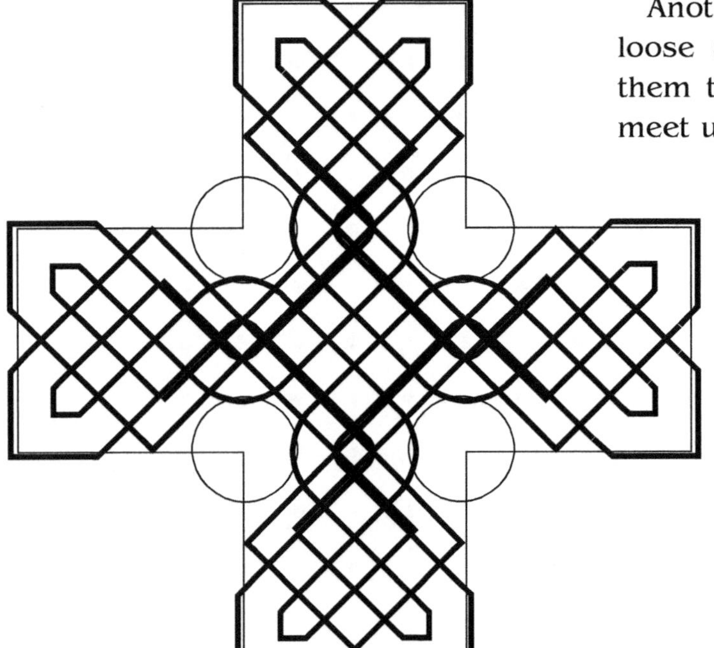

Another solution would be to bounce those loose strands off the outline edge and cross them through the center of the cross, so they meet up with the opposite strand. This makes a very interesting, complex design. Here I had to narrow the new crossing strands so they'd pass through the rest of the knotwork strands easily, which is a consideration that sometimes needs to be made when working out a design. The dots have been removed in this example to make it easier to see what was done.

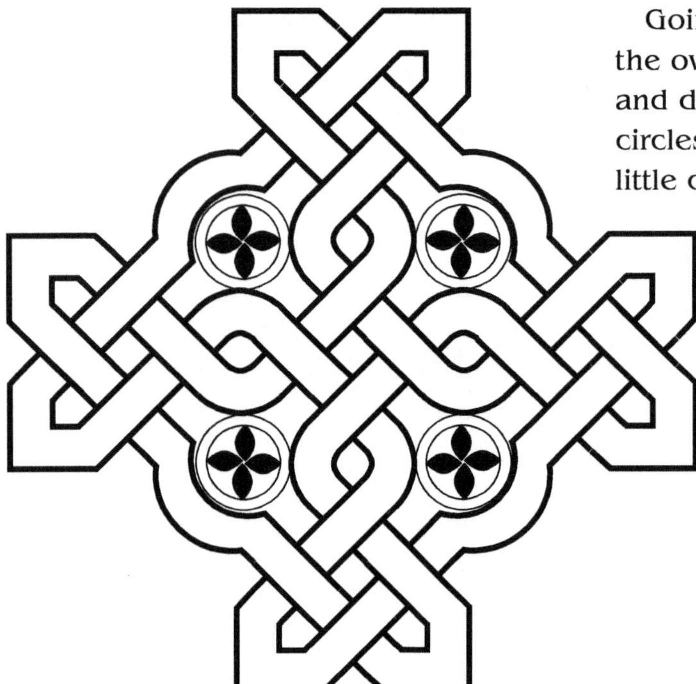

Going back to our first design, I've woven up the overs and unders, removed the cross outline and dots, and added some detail within my little circles. Even this simple solution made a lovely little cross.

The Ringed Cross

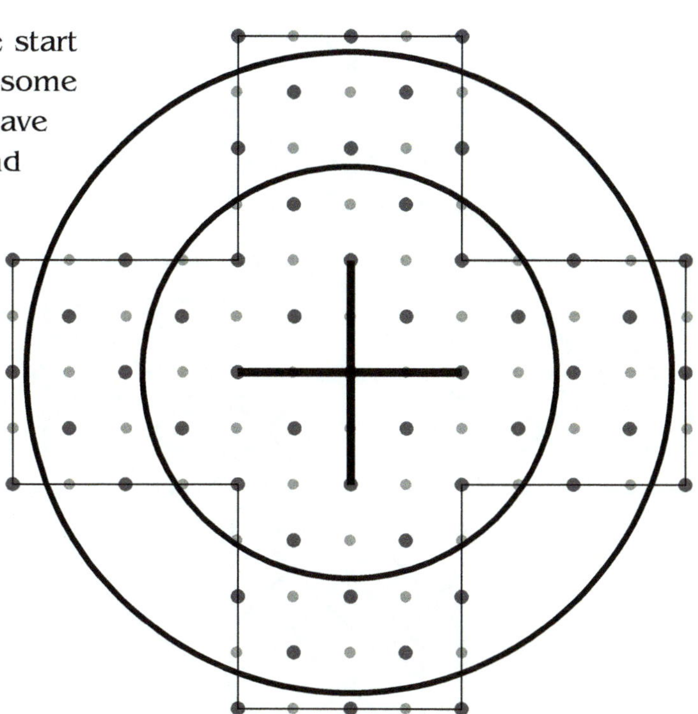

Now let's make a ringed cross. Again, we start with our basic cross shape and I've added some walls in the center for interest. After you have made your cross, mark off two circles around the center, one slightly larger than the other. As long as the first circle clears the armpits of the cross, the second circle can be any amount larger than the smaller circle that you want. These big rings can go through any dots because we will be freehanding the knots within them.

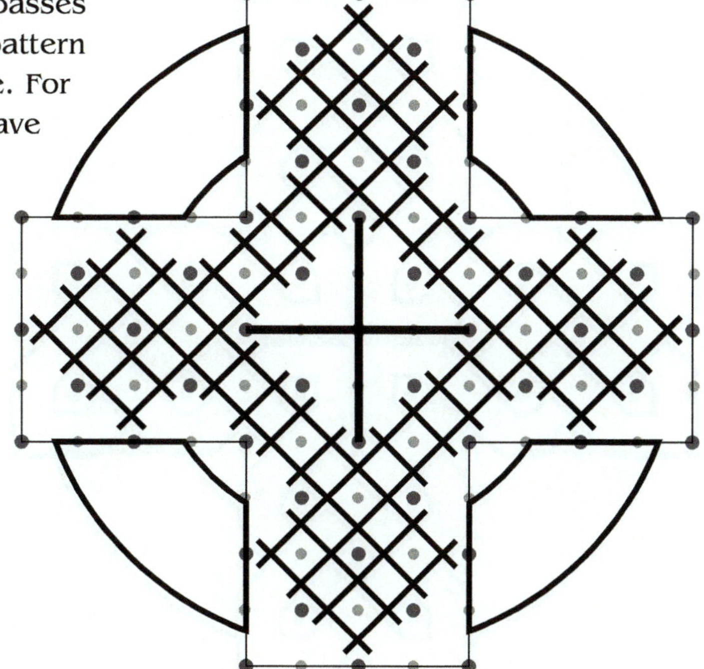

The circle has been erased where it passes over the cross. I've also added my "X" pattern over the small dots within the cross shape. For now, we will just deal with the cross and leave the circle segments for later.

CROSSES

The Ringed Cross...

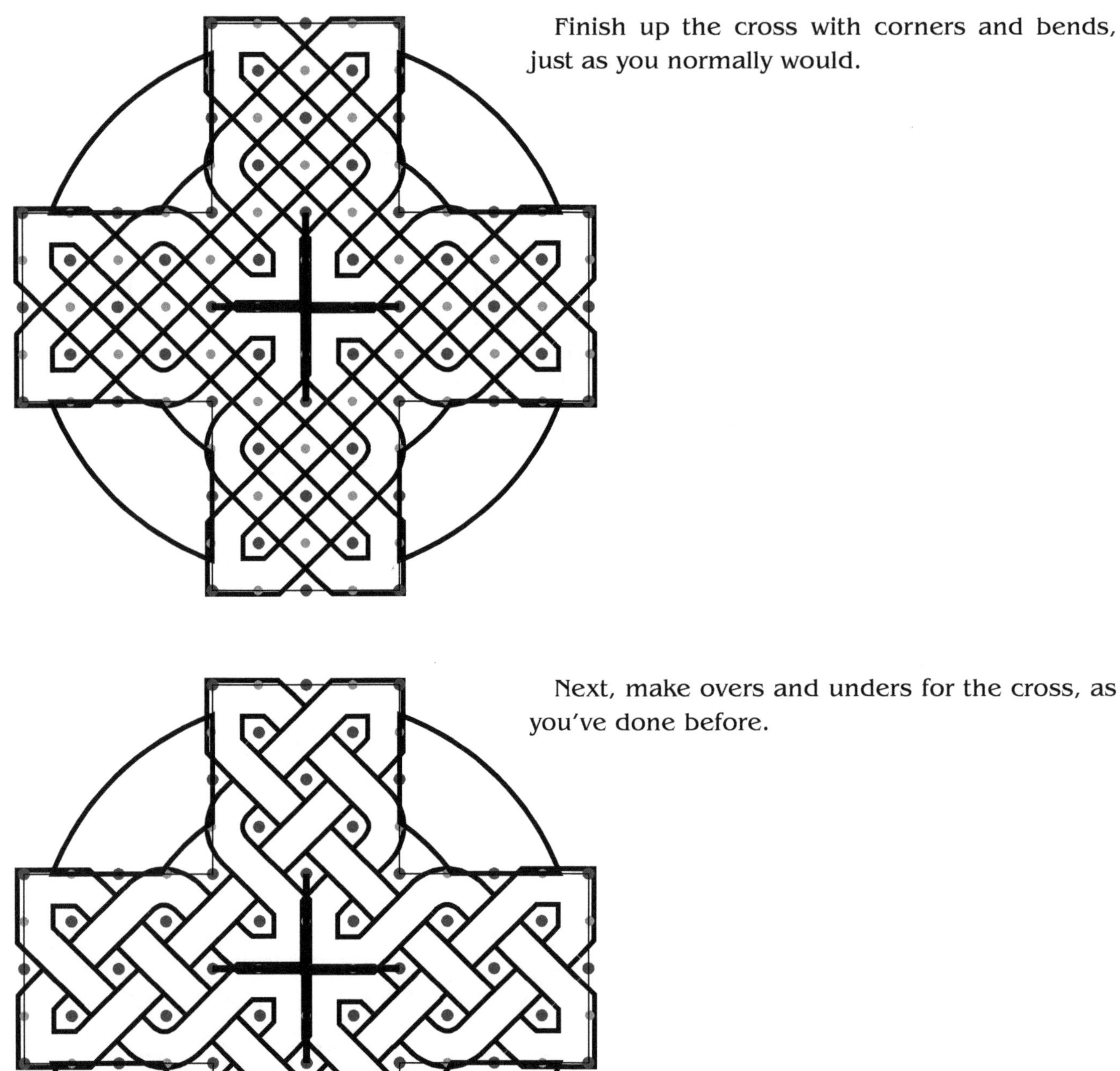

Finish up the cross with corners and bends, just as you normally would.

Next, make overs and unders for the cross, as you've done before.

The Ringed Cross...

Now comes the fun part. I'm going to make a knot within each of the four circle segments. To do this, I make a pointed oblong shape going from corner to corner in one of the ring sections. I make an echo of this shape inside it, so it's a double strand.

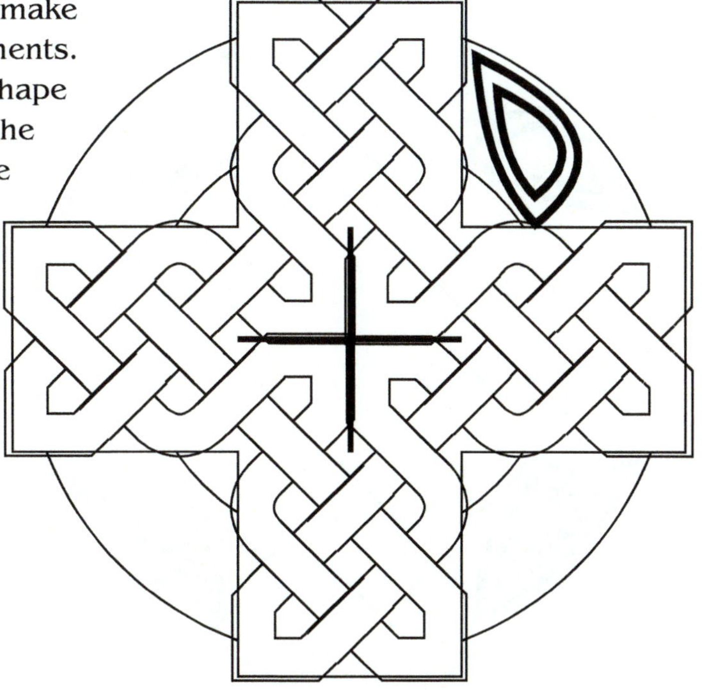

Then I make a second pair of pointed oblongs going from the remaining two corners, to mirror the first one.

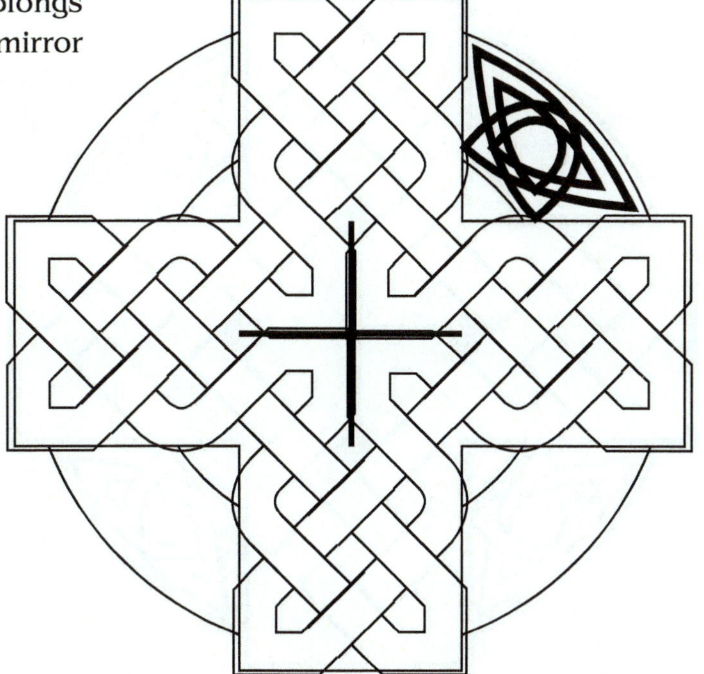

The Ringed Cross...

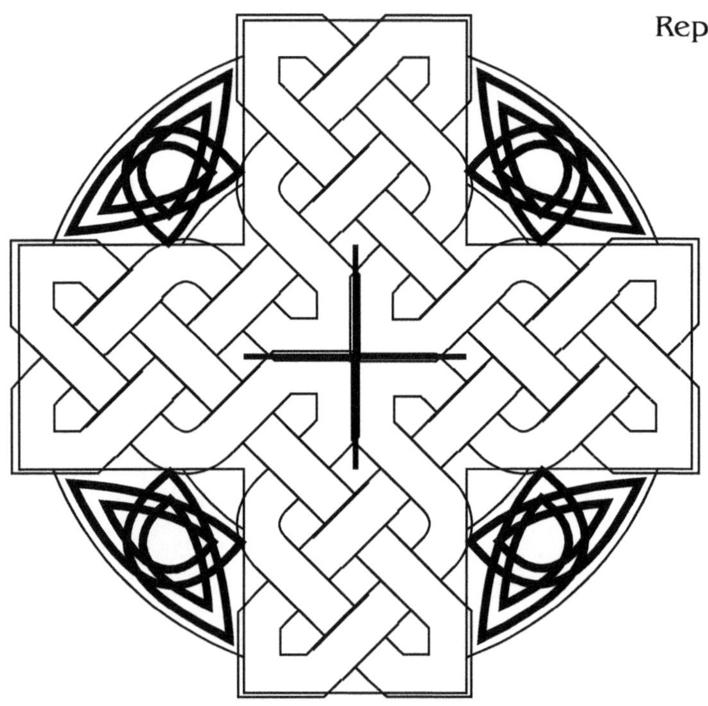

Repeat this shape in all four ring sections.

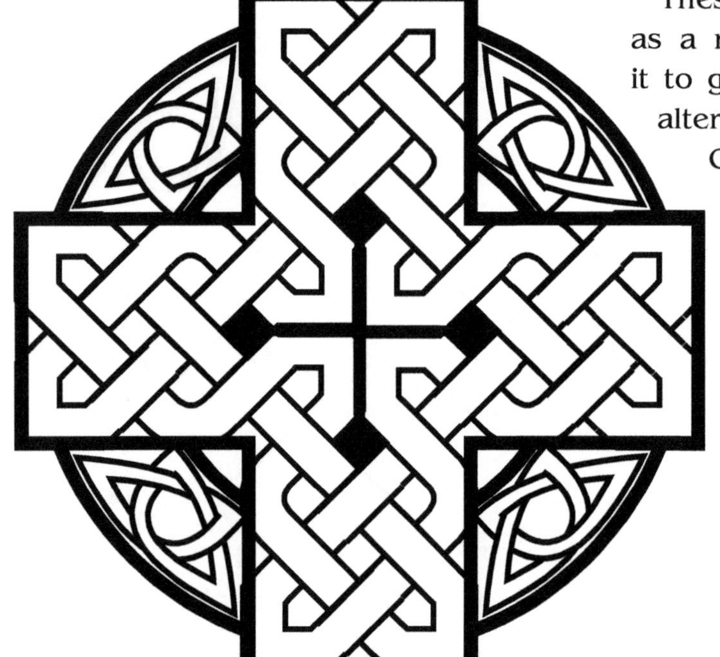

These freehand knots are woven the same way as a regular knot. Pick an intersection, erase it to go over or under, and then follow along, alternating the over-under pattern.

Once woven, I can make my outlines darker for dramatic effect and add some dark diamonds within the center for interest.

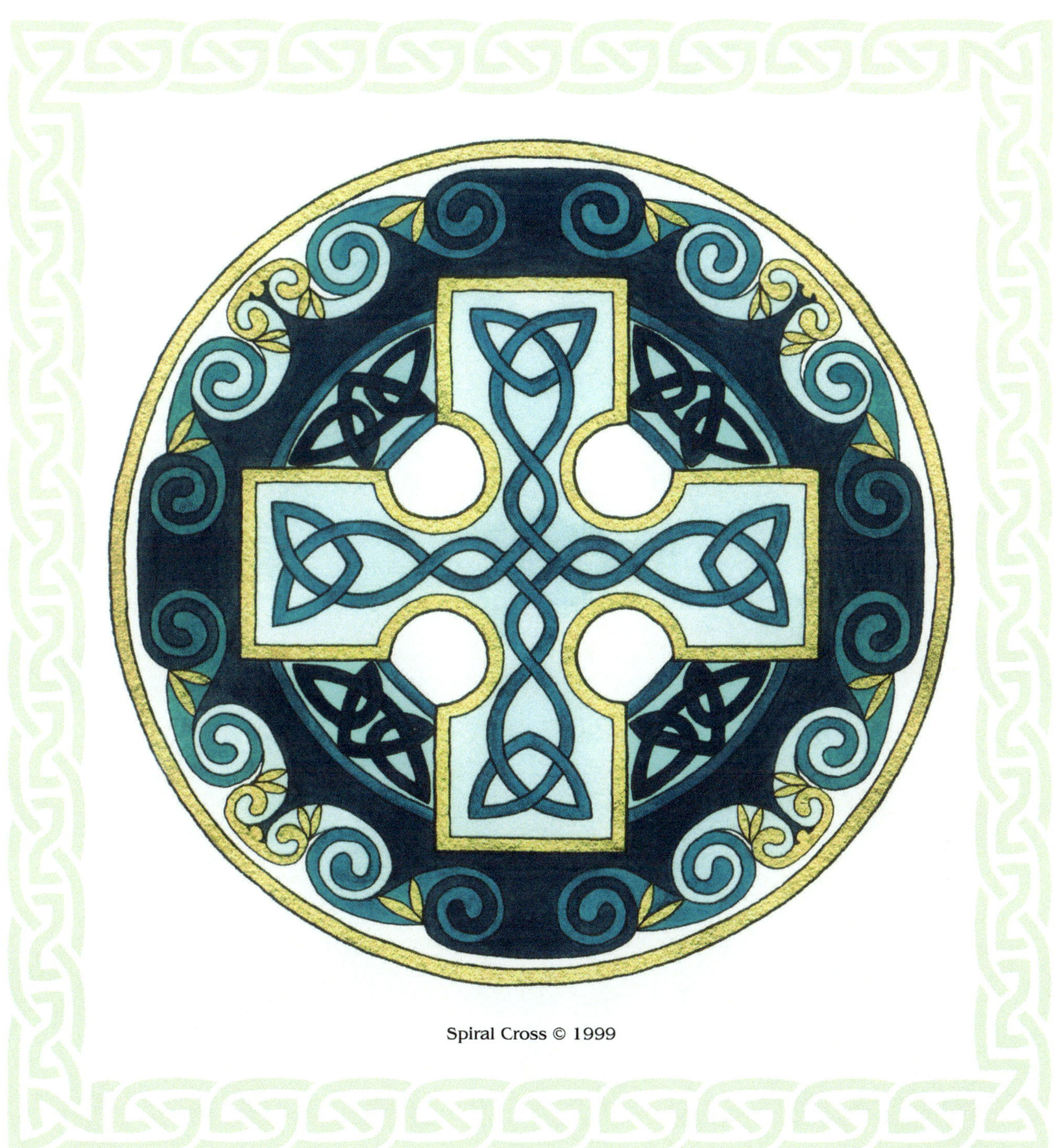

Spiral Cross © 1999

SPIRALS

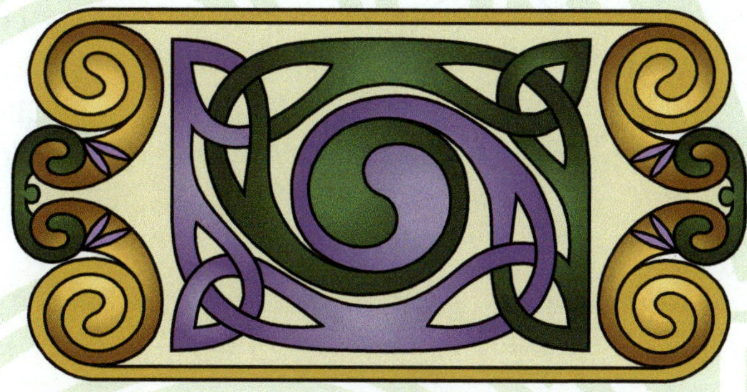

Celtic Spirals

Double Spirals

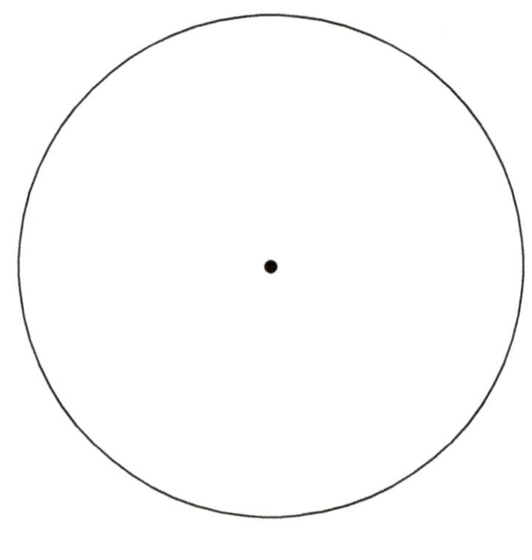

One way to make a Spiral is by using a compass, but I find that process slow and frustrating. Here I'll show you how I freehand draw my Spirals. While it takes a bit of practice to get the spiral even, I think it works out to be a faster way of drawing them in the end.

To start a Spiral, first mark off a circle on plain paper using a compass or circle template. Mark the middle of your circle.

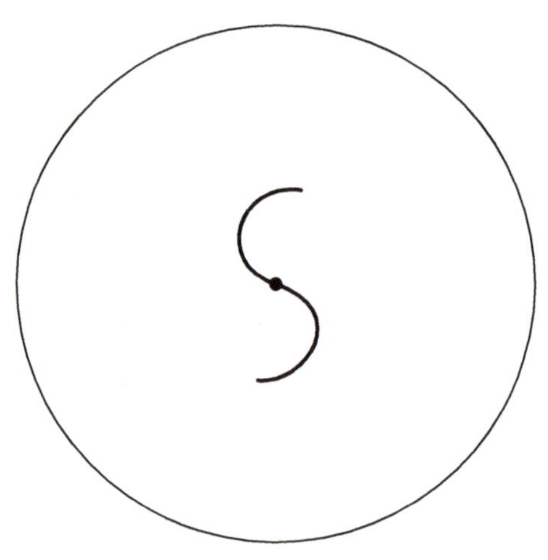

Begin your Spiral by making an "S" shape inside the circle. Make sure that the center of the "S" passes through the center mark of your circle. Both the upper half and the lower half of the "S" should be even curves of approximately the same size.

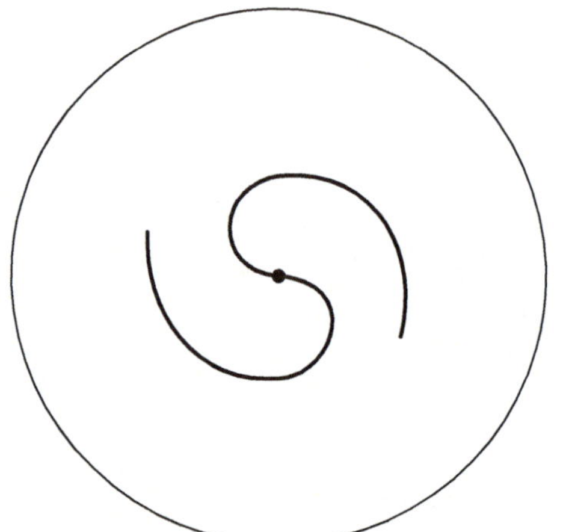

A Spiral is made up of two parts. The head is the large, round part in the center and the tail is the long, tapered part that winds its way around the head. In the example to the left, we've started the heads. The next step is to taper the tails around the two heads.

Choose one free end and draw it a little way around the circle. Do the same with the other tail.

Celtic Spirals...

Continue to curl each tail around, trying to keep the space between the tail and the outer circle about equal. As you continue, the tails will automatically taper and get thinner and thinner. Try to extend each tail by the same distance each time and alternate between them so they grow at the same rate.

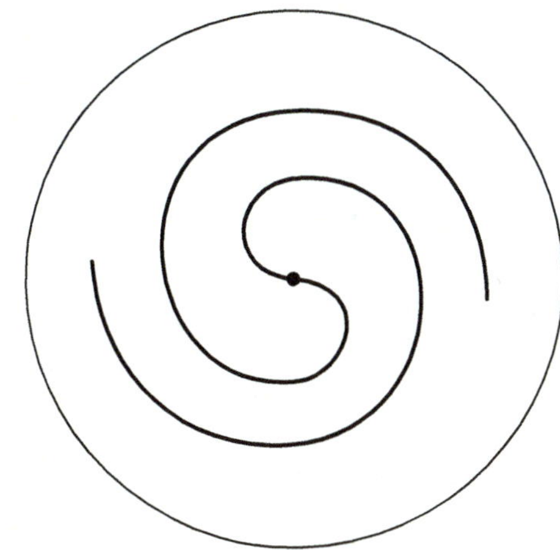

Continue to follow the tails around, closer and closer to the outer circle.

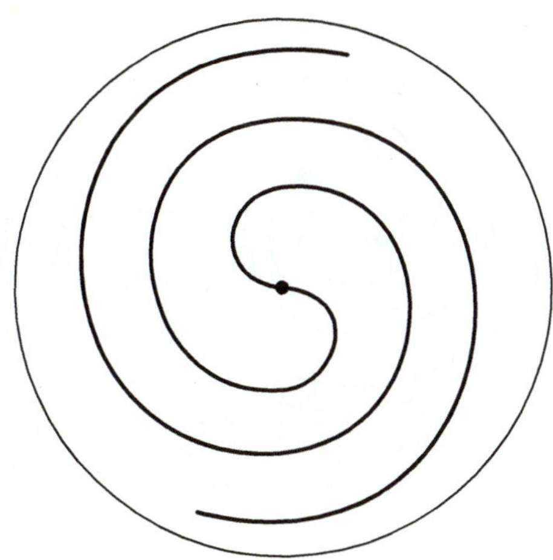

The tails will naturally meet up with the outer circle and complete the spiral.

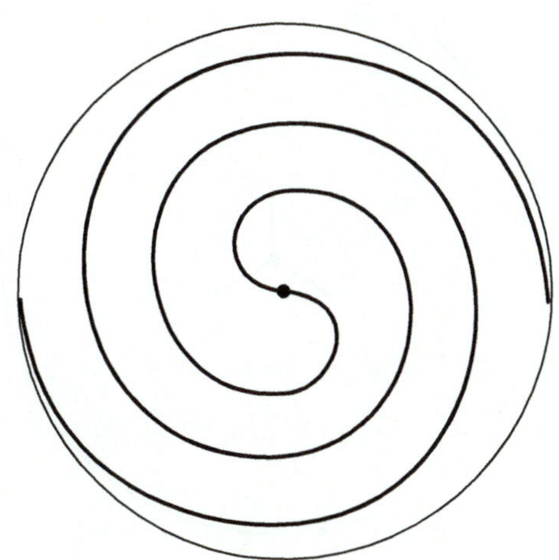

Celtic Spirals...

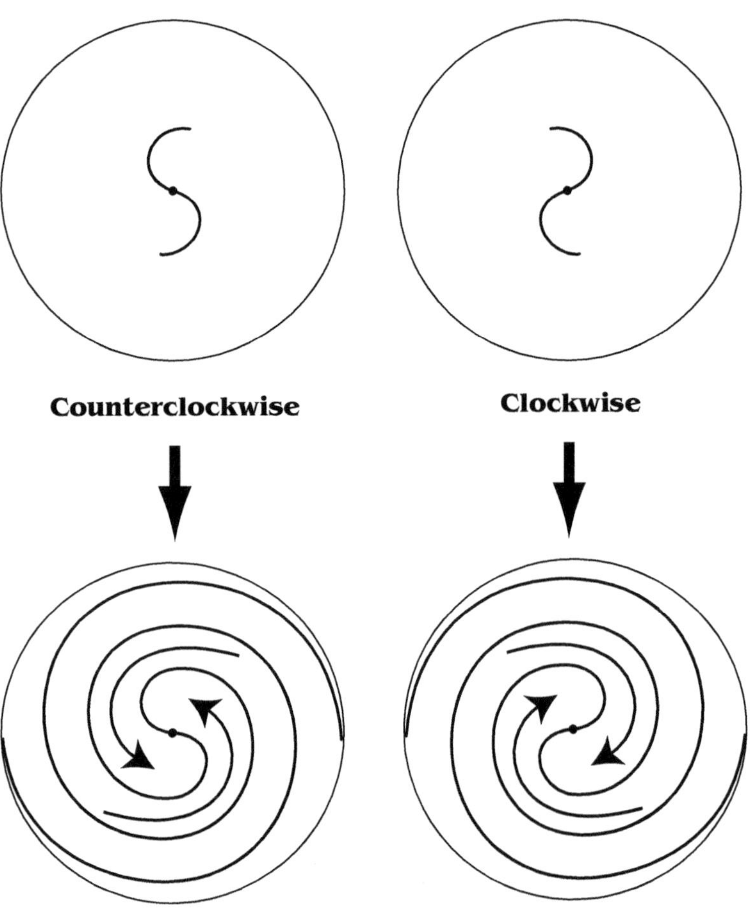

Spirals can curl clockwise or counterclockwise. Some sources may claim that one direction or the other is "correct" in terms of Celtic art, but that isn't true. Historical examples can be found of spirals going in either direction, especially when patterns have been created that join them together and they are used to fill spaces. To reverse the direction of a spiral, all you need to do is reverse the direction of the "S" and then wind it up normally.

Triple Spirals

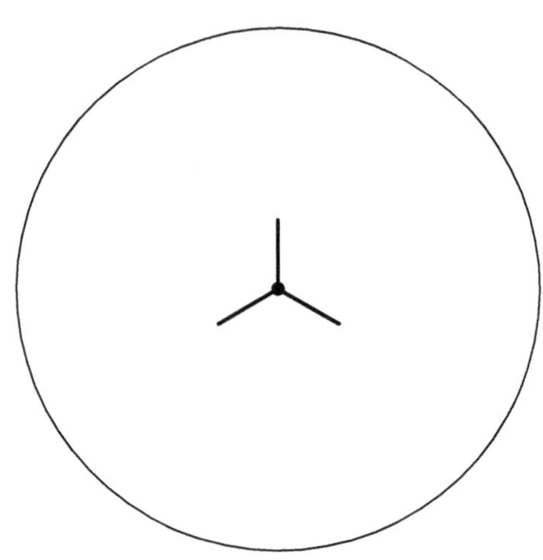

To make a triple Celtic Spiral, begin with a circle again. In the center of the circle, make a small "Y" shape. It doesn't have to extend very far, but make sure that each arm of the "Y" extends about 120 degrees from the other to divide the circle into three equal portions.

Celtic Spirals...

Add a "scoop" shape to the end of each "Y" arm. Make sure that the scoops all face the same direction around the circle.

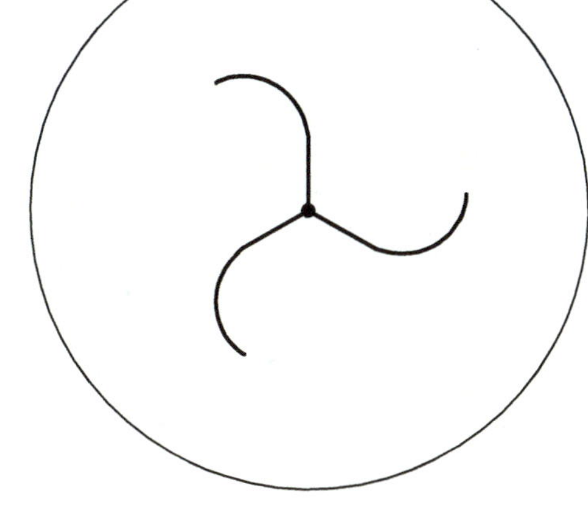

Each tail should be drawn a short length at a time, making sure to draw the same amount on each tail as you continue. They should begin to curl around your scoops (the heads of the spirals). Slowly extend the tails around the heads, one tail at a time.

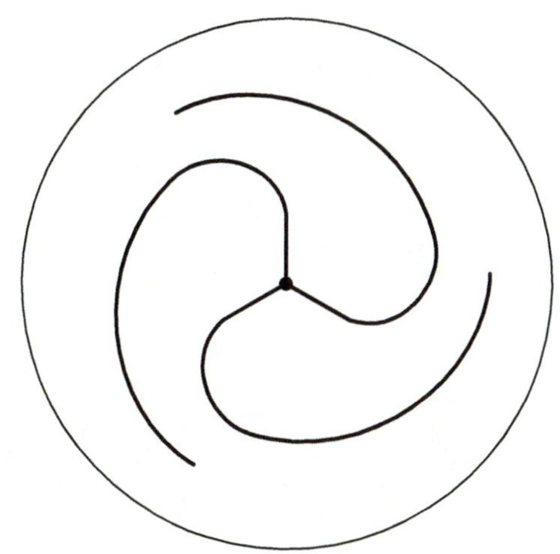

Continue drawing the tails until they meet up naturally with the outer circle.

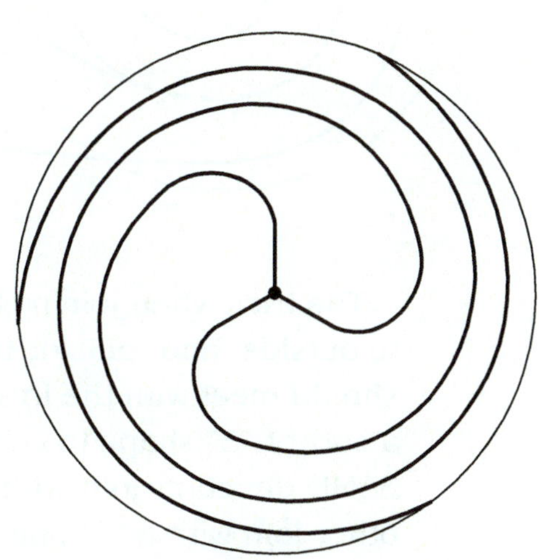

Celtic Spirals...

Joining Spirals

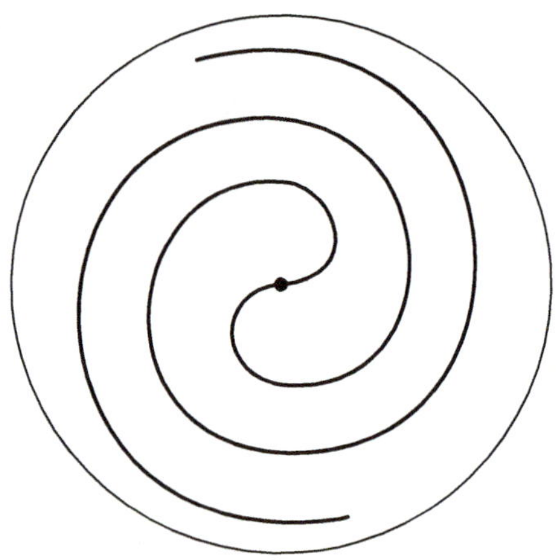
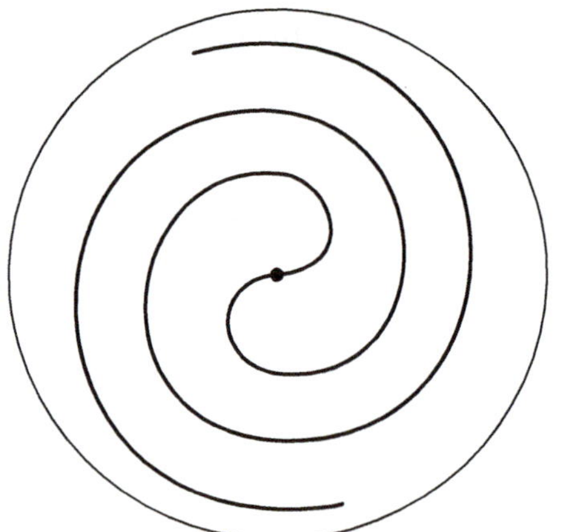

Joining two Spirals is pretty simple. First start with two spirals a short distance apart from each other. Position them so that their tails taper off at the top or bottom. For this example ensure they're both spinning in the same direction.

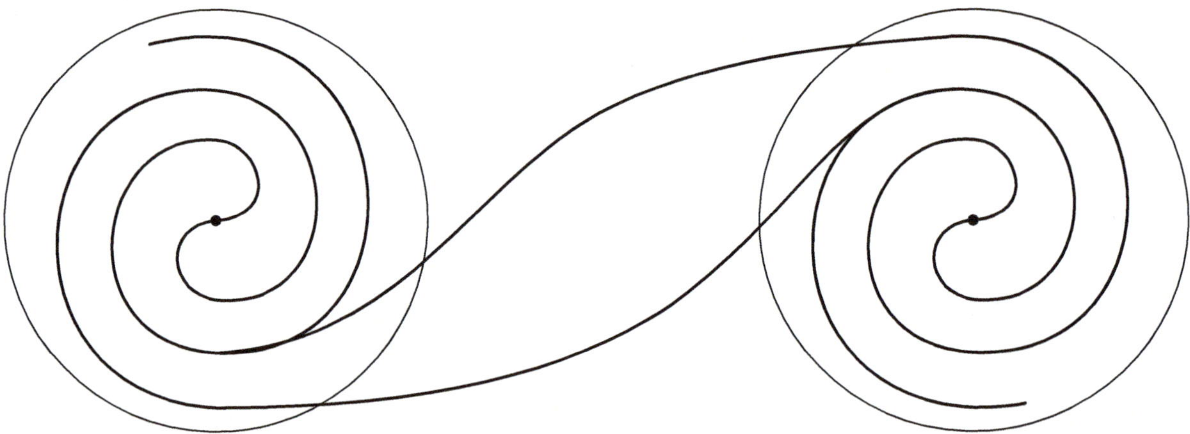

The trick when joining two spirals spinning in the SAME direction is "inside to outside" and "outside to inside." So the OUTSIDE free tail leaving one spiral should meet with the INSIDE line of the other spiral and vice versa. It makes a sort of "S" shape to connect them. To remember it, spirals spinning in the SAME direction join with an "S" shape. Spirals spinning COUNTER to each other join with a "C" shape (see the end of the chapter for an illustration).

Celtic spirals...

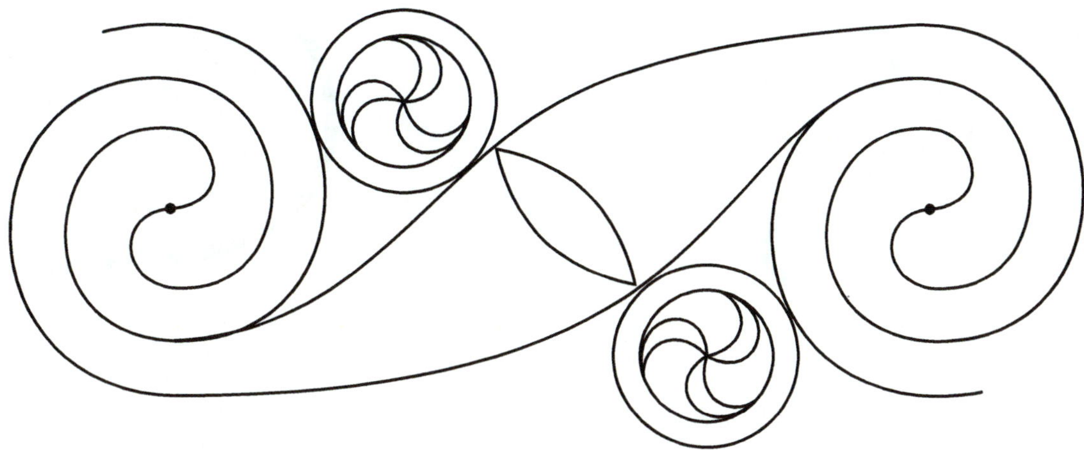

Gaps around the spirals and their joins can be filled with simple shapes or even knotwork. The triangle shape is ideal for adding trefoil knots!

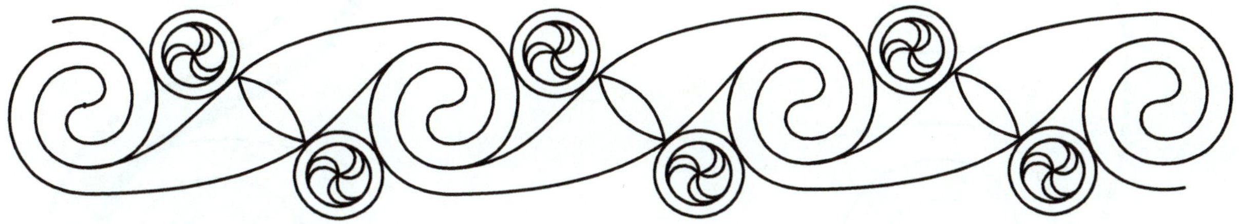

If desired, attach the loose ends to more spirals to make a border, or arc them to make a ring—whatever you want. If you want a stand-alone design, try attaching the loose ends of one spiral to the other so it's all connected and whole.

Celtic spirals...

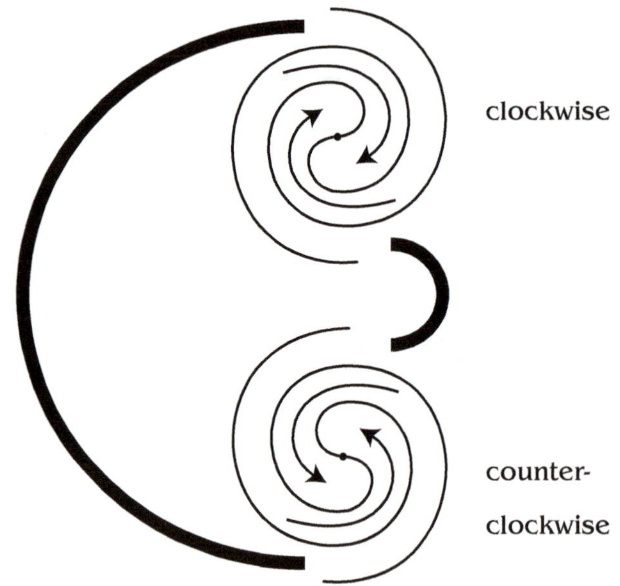

Counter Spin = **C** join

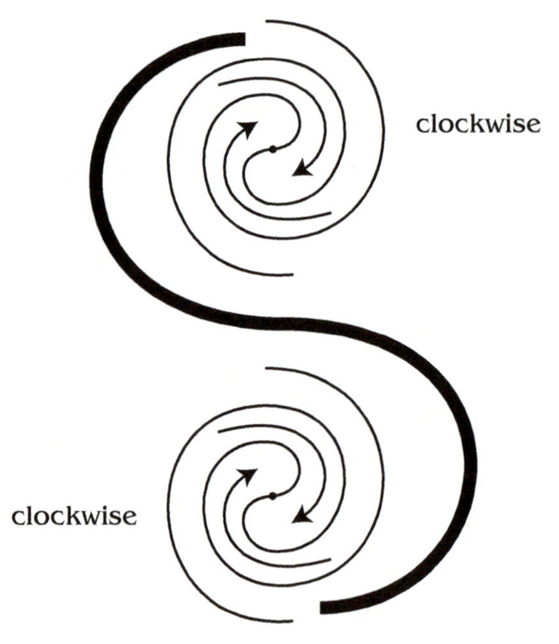

Same Spin = **S** join

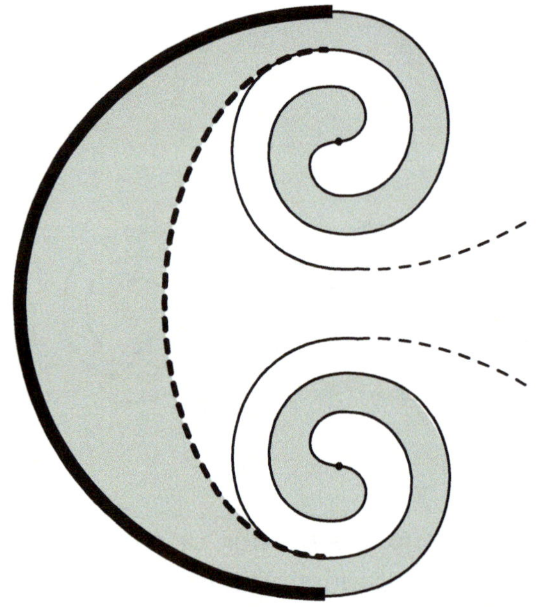

C join: inside to inside, outside to outside.

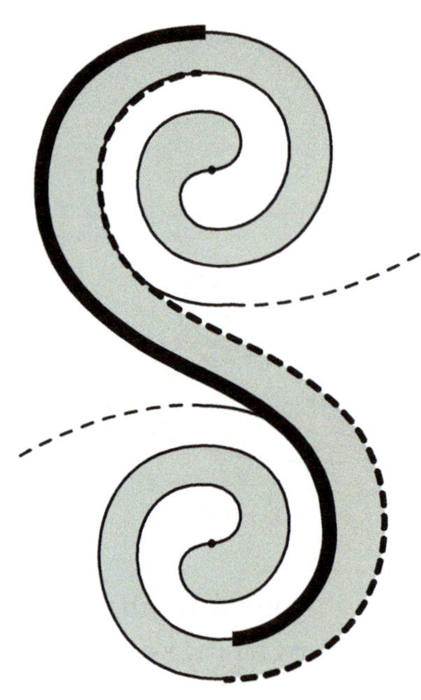

S join: outside to inside, inside to outside.

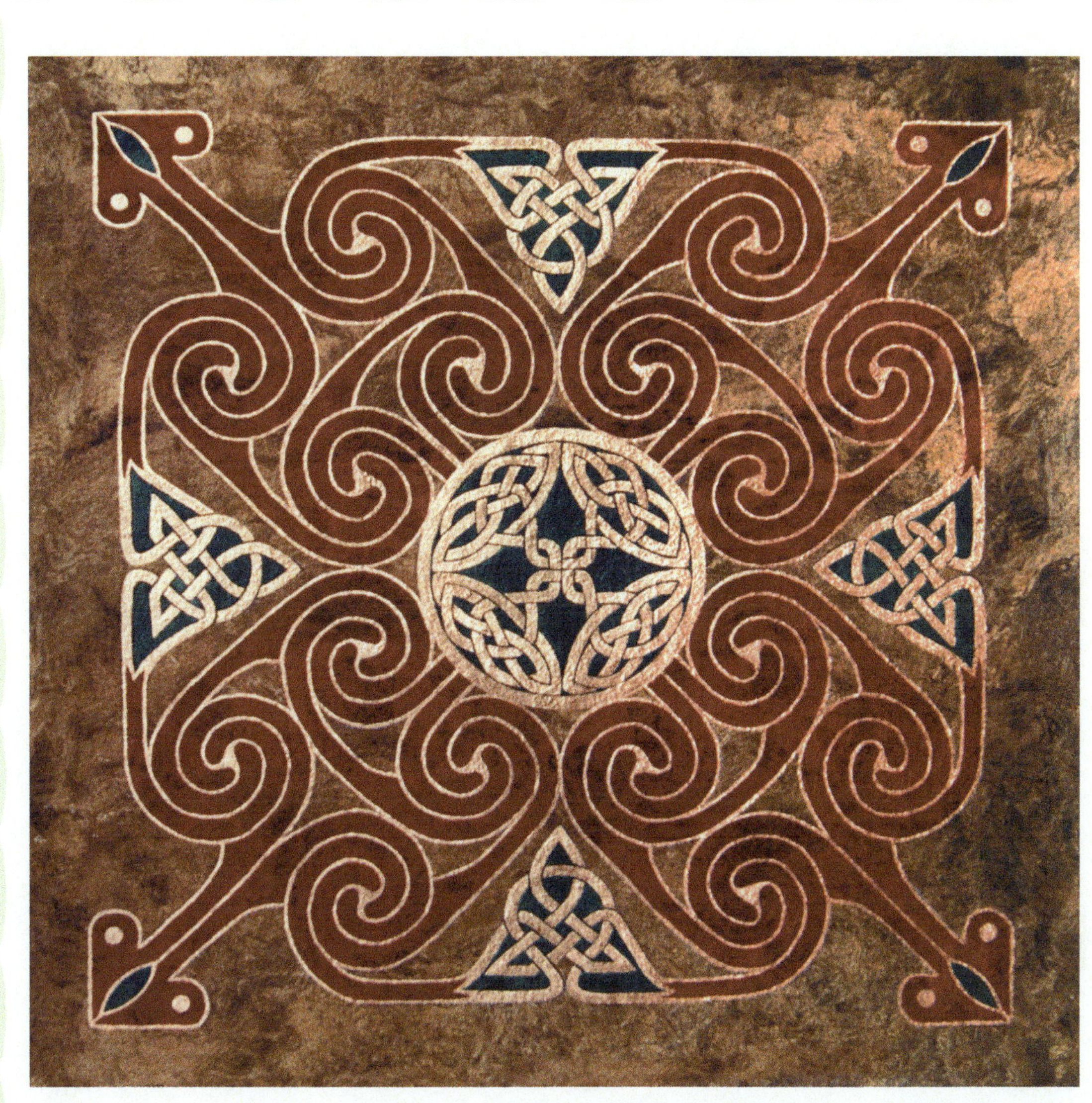

Copper Knot © 1995

MAZE & STEP PATTERNS

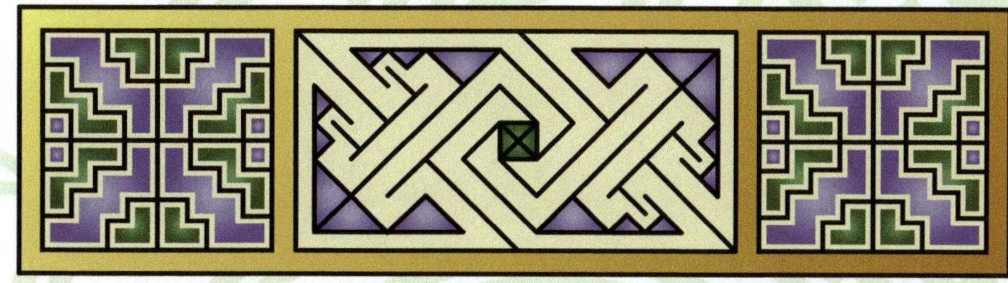

Maze Patterns

A common pattern found in ancient Celtic art is the Maze pattern. It was used as a filler for large blank spaces and also as a pattern within other Celtic designs, such as knots and spirals. The Maze pattern resembles old-fashioned labyrinths and can be used to create sacred labyrinth designs as well.

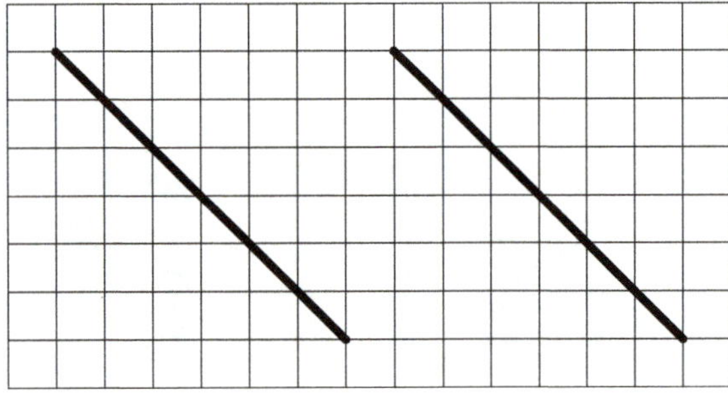

Maze patterns are mostly easily created with graph paper. For this example, mark off an area that's 8 x 15 squares on the graph paper. In this area, make two diagonal lines, as shown. The lines should not connect with an outer boundary box. It is not always essential to start the next diagonal over by one square as I did here. It can begin a few squares over or the ends can be directly above each other, depending on what you want to do.

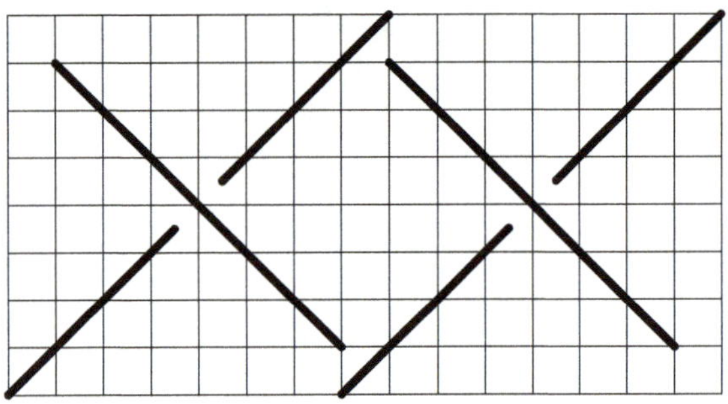

Now we add some diagonals going in the other direction, but start these from the edges of the marked-off box. Break these diagonals in the middle so they don't cross over the first lines. A good way to remember this is: if the line touches the edges of the marked-off area, then it breaks in the middle; if it DOESN'T touch the edges, then it goes through the middle. It can only be one way or the other; one type of line shouldn't do both (touch the edge and pass through the middle).

Maze patterns...

Next, we add some arrowheads to the loose ends. The arrowhead ends shouldn't connect with any lines because we want to make sure there is an open channel running through the Maze or labyrinth. Just extend them a way and then stop at least a square away from another line.

In the example, the inner arrowhead lines are quite short so there is room for some different turns in the center of the design.

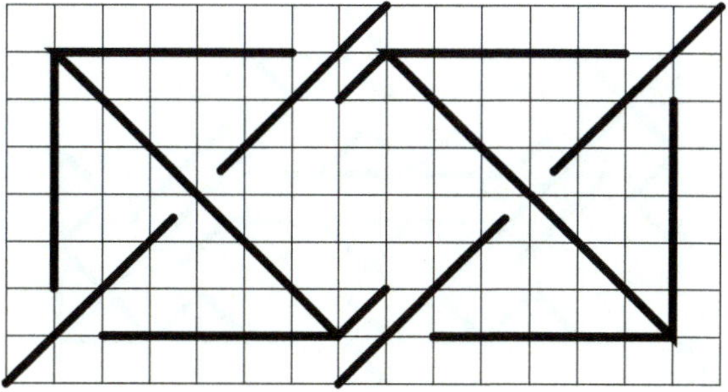

Now I have added some more arrowhead shapes, again making sure to not connect anything but to leave a little gap at the ends of the arrowhead lines.

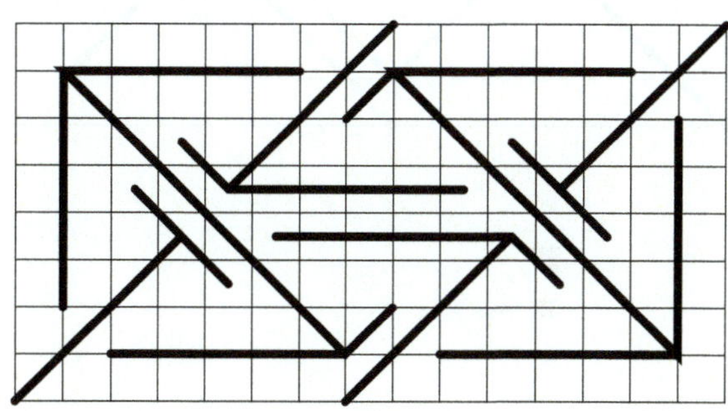

Maze patterns...

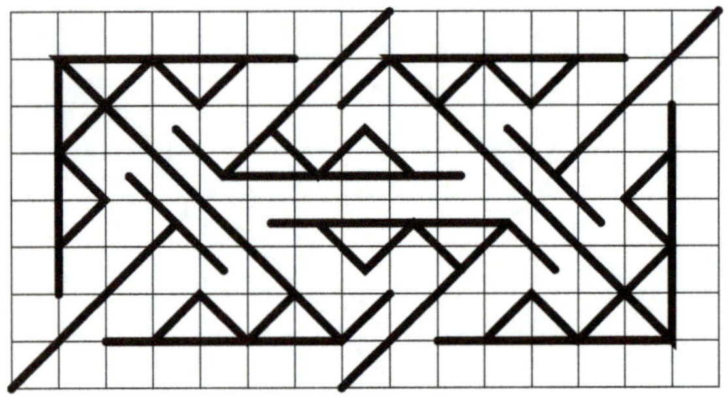

Triangles are used to add detail to Maze designs. In the example I've added little triangles to the longer halves of the arrowheads and to the corners of the design. Add triangles to your pattern to break up the open spaces.

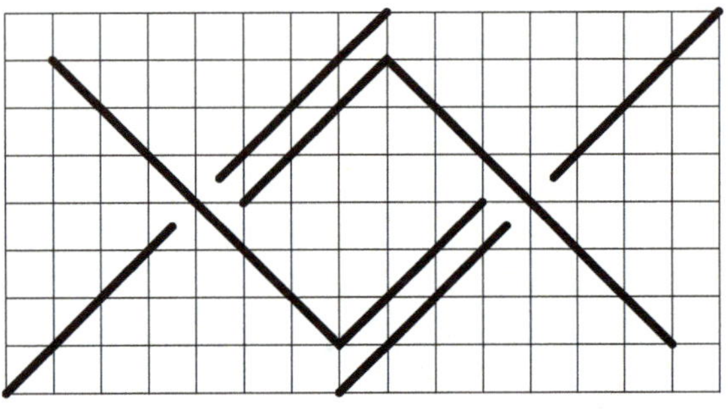

This example shows a different treatment of the same design. The pattern begins in the same way as the last one, only this time we are going to make a square spiral design in the center.

First, start where the first half of the arrowhead we just made joins with the arrow stem, then draw a line into the middle of the design, about three squares across, from each end.

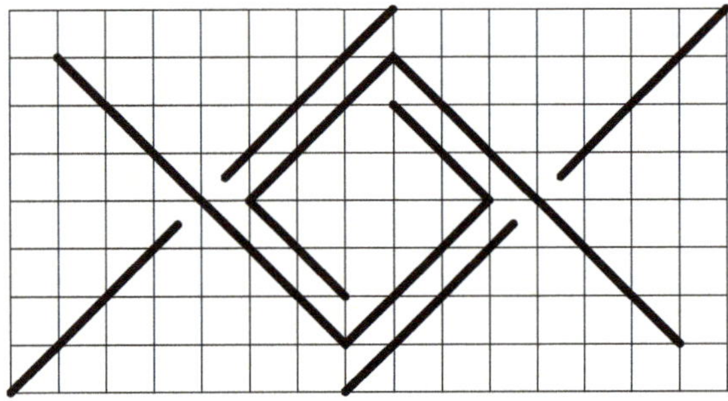

Continue this line from each side by drawing a line that is two squares across.

Maze patterns...

Continue the line again by drawing each into the design more, by one square this time, and then attaching the ends so the spiral is complete.

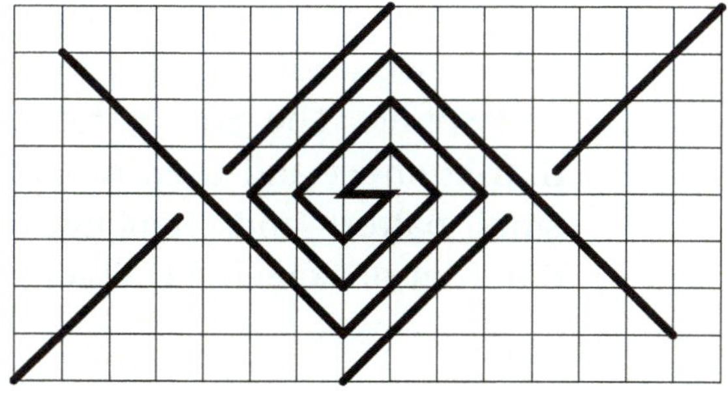

Add ends to the other lines. I could change the ways I add the arrowheads to the lines, but I'll keep it fairly close to the original example so you can see the difference.

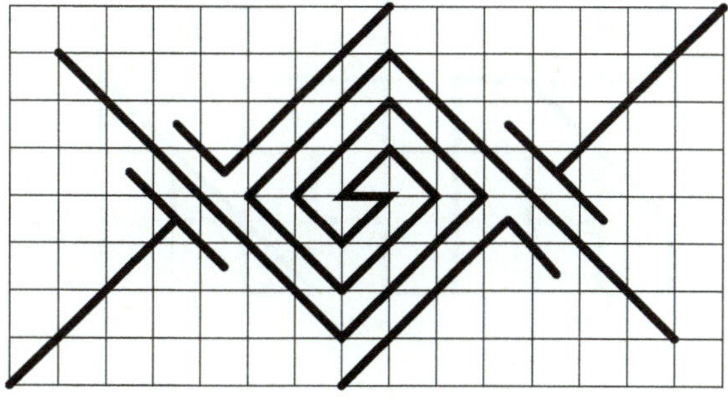

Finally add triangles to the design to fill the open spaces. Here I've made some of the triangles bigger around the spiral design while leaving the rest of the triangles the same size.

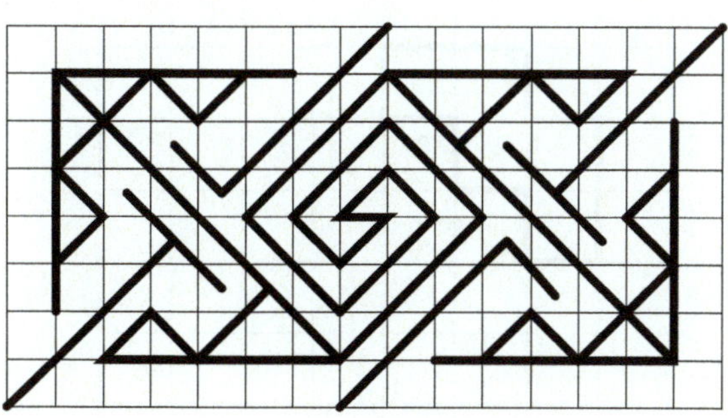

Step Patterns

Another common pattern in ancient Celtic art is the Step or Tile pattern. It was also used as a filler for large blank spaces or as a pattern within knots and spirals. The Step pattern looks like it's made up of small tile shapes that connect and then repeat to form a larger pattern. By starting with a small pattern and changing the way you repeat it, you can create a lot of different designs really quickly.

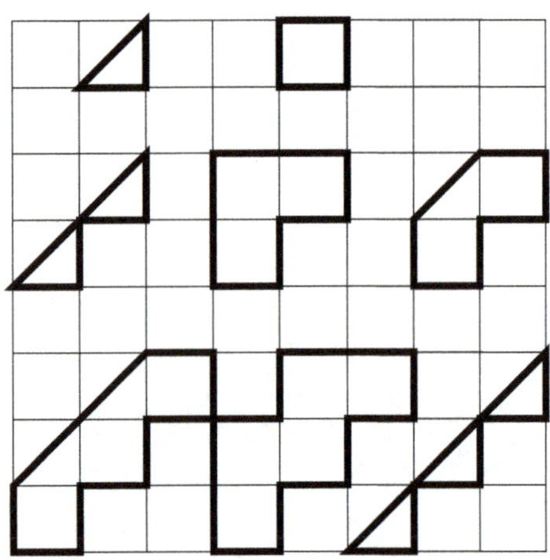

To the left I've drawn some of the common shapes used, but experiment with your own or mix and match. On the top row are some simple pieces, a small triangle and a square. The next row has "V" shapes and variations on those. The third row has "W" shapes.

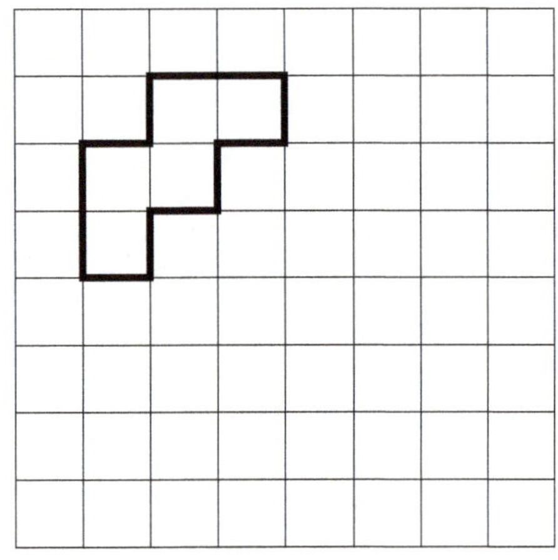

This first shape is a "W". Place this somewhere in the top corner, leaving enough room so more can be added to the tile in the next step.

Step patterns...

To finish the 3 x 3 tile, I have added a square piece to one corner of the "W" and a "V" piece to the other. Notice how they all lock together to form an interesting pattern.

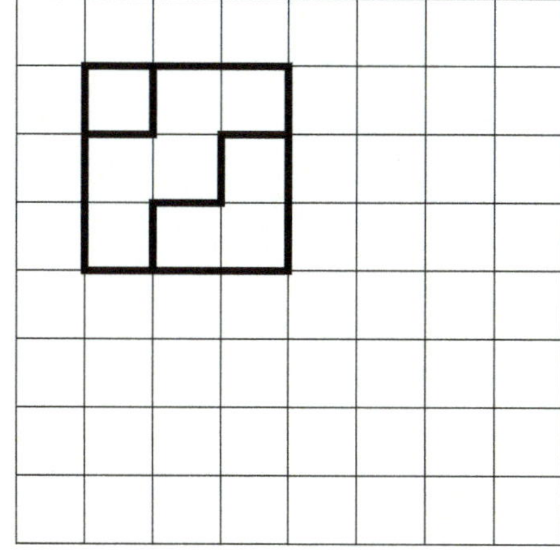

Now rotate copies of the little tile to make a larger tile.

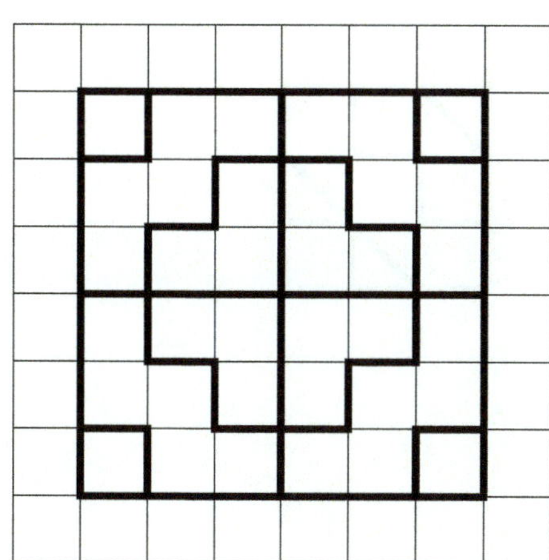

An entirely different design can be created of the original tile if it is turned around before repeating it. One small tile can be used to make all kinds of different patterns depending on how you turn the little tiles and how you join them up.

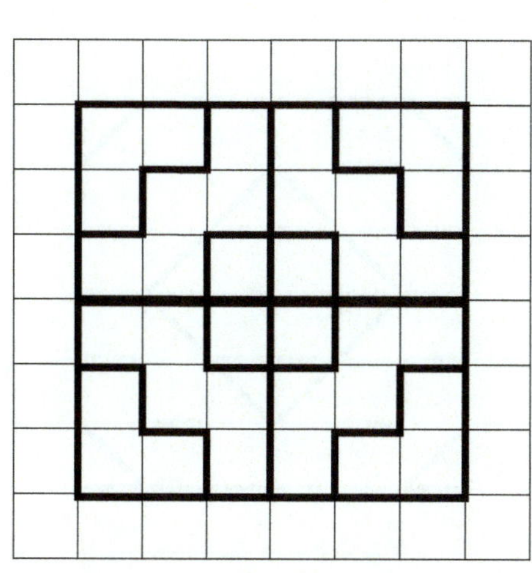

Step patterns...

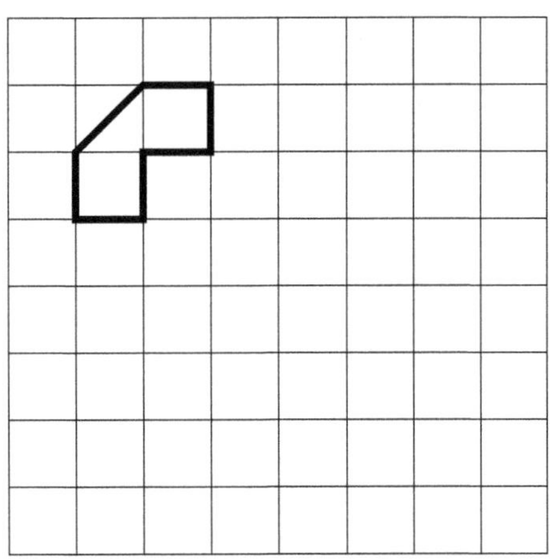

For this example, I'll start with a "V" shape variation.

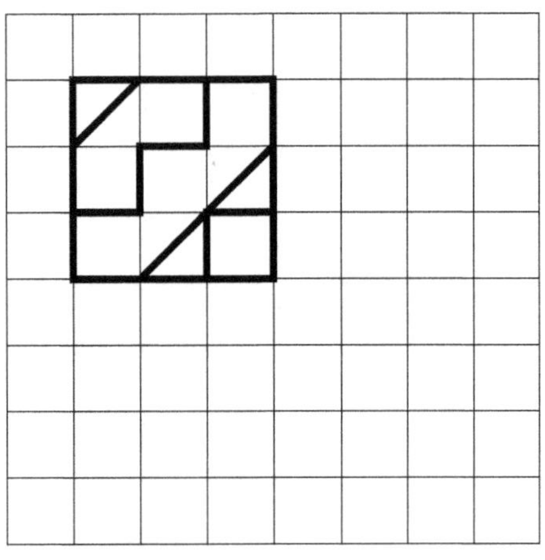

To fill the small spot where my "V" is missing its point, I've added a small triangle shape and plugged one of the "W" shapes into the other side of the "V", then filled in the "W" with more triangles. It may seem like you are adding a lot of shapes for no reason in your little tile, but keep in mind that the more little sections and divisions you make, the more areas you'll have in your final pattern to color!

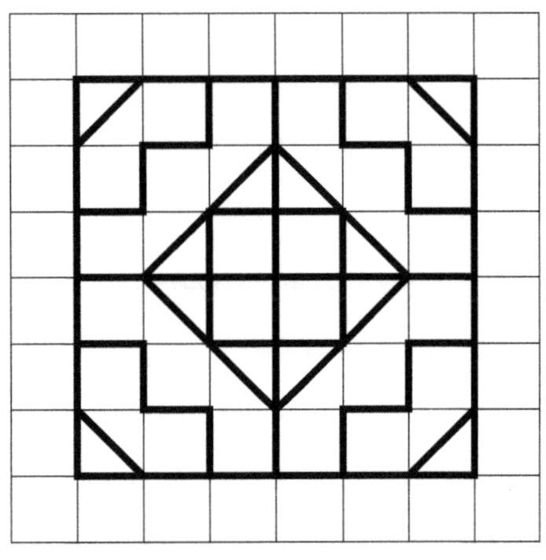

As before, rotate the little tile to get a bigger tile. This bigger tile, if you want to make a really big pattern, may be rotated again and made into an even larger tile.

Step patterns...

Here I took that little tile and gave it a turn before rotating a copy of it around, giving the larger tile a totally different look.

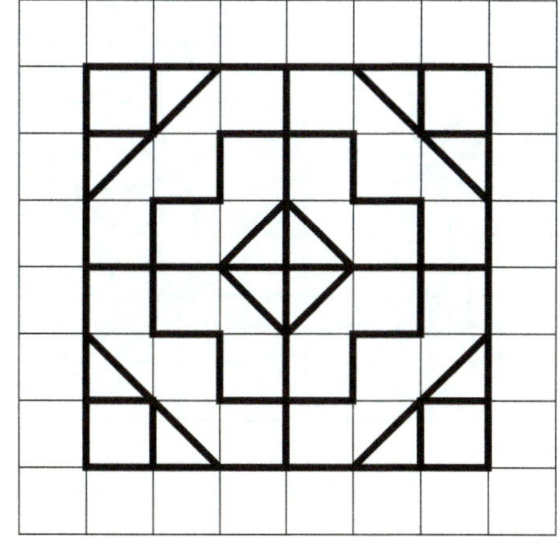

You can also integrate both Maze and Step patterns into a single overall design, as both are based on a grid of squares for their layout.

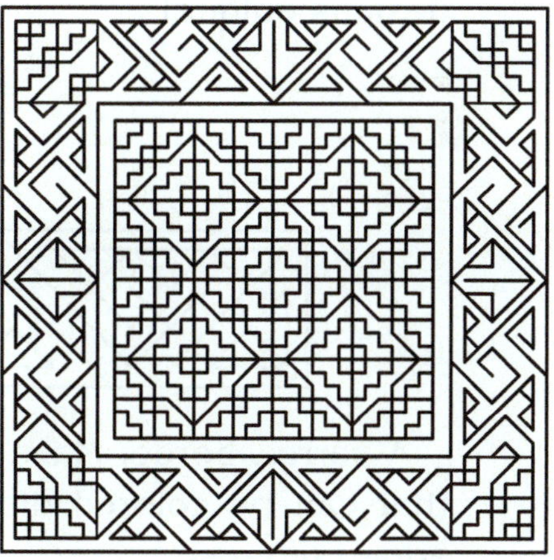

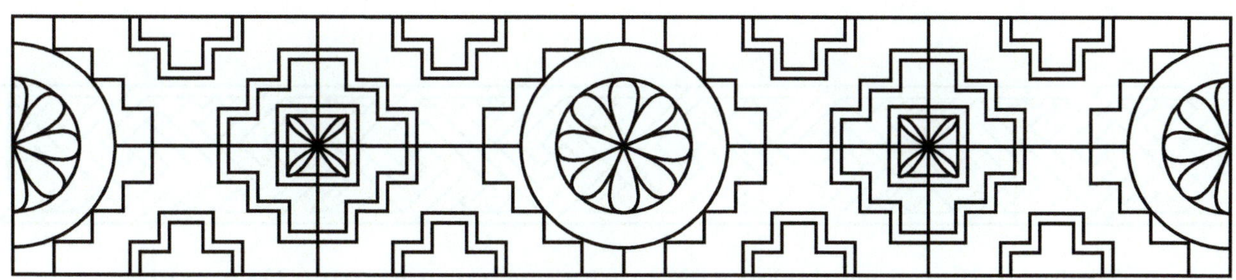

With the basics of this idea, it's possible to create complex designs easily. Here some thinner double outlines have been added to some of my squares for coloring purposes later on. Daisies have also been added to the design to make it more interesting.

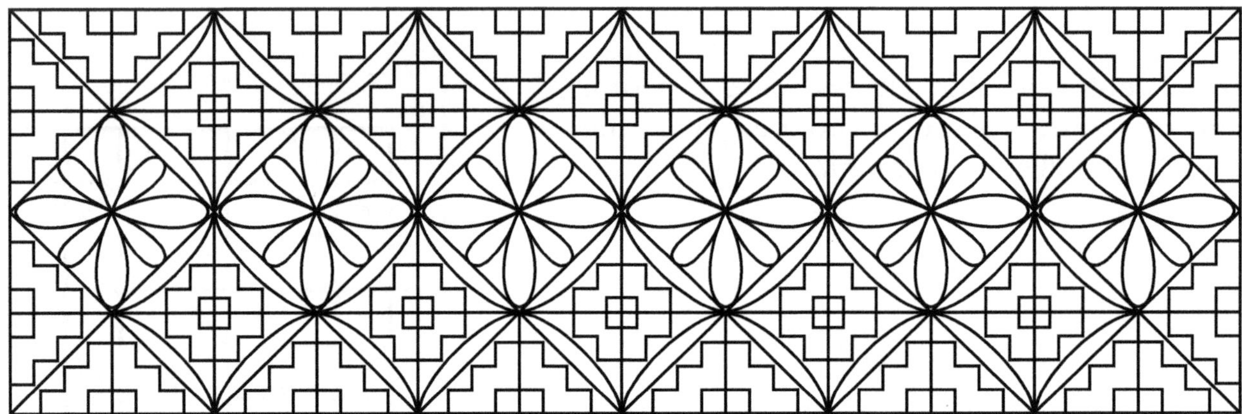

In this example, freehanded flowers fill the central sections to give some interest and break up the repeat of the pattern. Notice the half-moon shapes surrounding the flowers and branching between the steps of the pattern. Don't be afraid to mix and match style elements to make your designs unique!

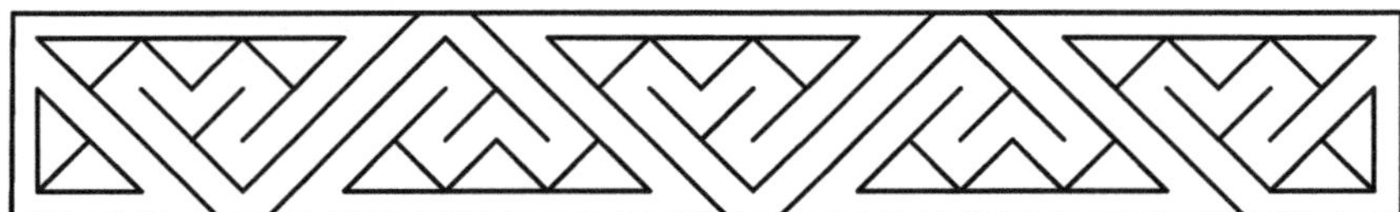

A narrow-border Maze design. Adding the triangle shapes creates areas that can be colored differently than the background of the design, for added interest.

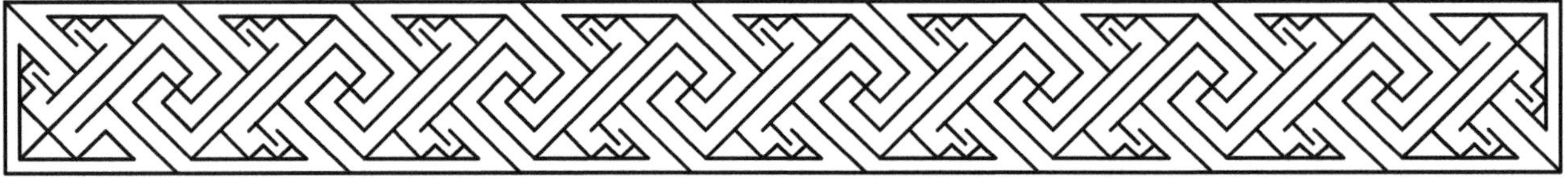

Similar to the above design, this border was created using Maze patterns over a larger area. The repeating swirl pattern ends up being a quadruple spiral, only this example is angular instead of rounded as was seen in the Spiral chapter.

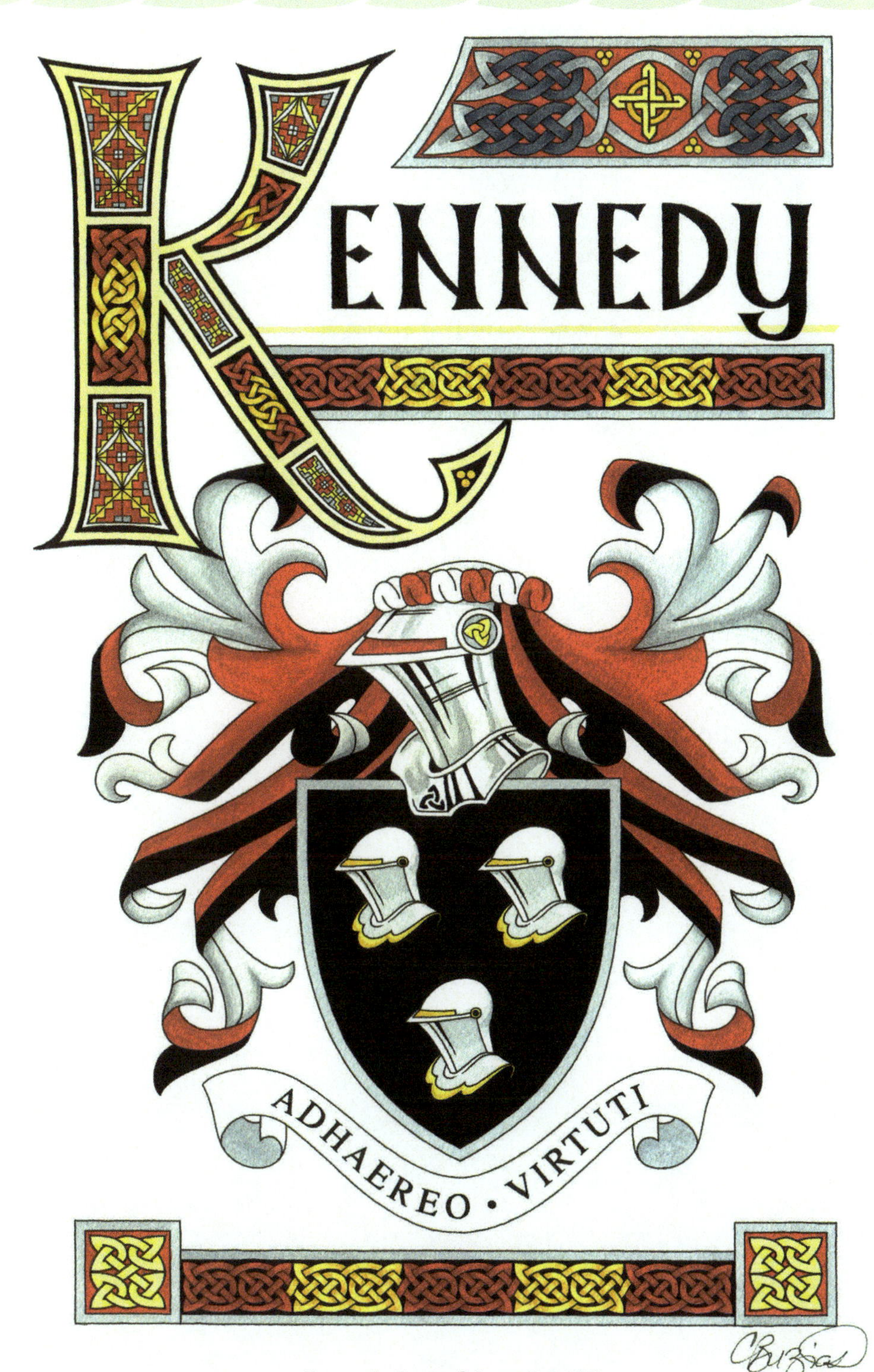

Kennedy Coat of Arms © 2006

ZOOMORPHICS

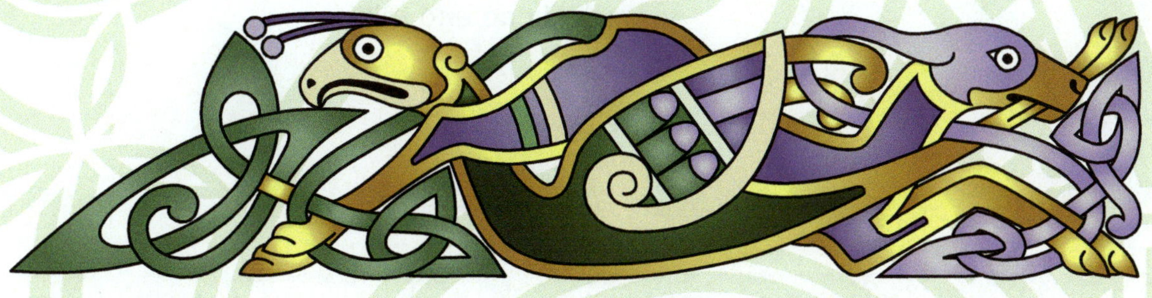

Snakes and Dragons

Snakes were frequently used in the old Celtic manuscripts such as the Book of Kells and Lindisfarne Gospels. Although you might be tempted to think that serpents in a bible might only be depicted in negative ways, that was certainly not the case. Serpents were added as illustrations just like any other animal and were perhaps graphically useful in that they could be created and woven into traditional knotwork.

Dragons were not typically drawn in historic Celtic art. Most of the "Celtic dragon" designs you see today are modern creations by artists, so when it comes to making your own Dragons, you have a lot of free rein. You can style your Dragon after other cultures—Chinese, Norse, Aztec—or make your own unique style.

This chapter covers how to turn a traditional Celtic Snake into a Dragon, and also how to take a knotwork design and transform it into a Dragon. With these two techniques you can jump-start your Dragon drawing using what you've already learned about drawing knots.

Snake-to-Dragon Transformation

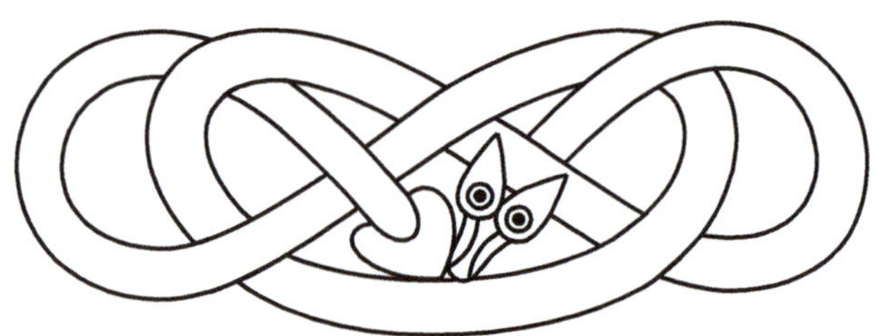

Here we have a traditional Snake design. He basically looks like a Celtic Knot but has a Celtic snake head and spade-shaped tail. You can pick any Celtic Snake for your Dragon transformation; however, make sure your source is not copyright protected before you copy it. Pretty much everything on the internet is copyright to someone, so it's best to work from a photo of an ancient manuscript or other authentic ancient source instead. The first step is to draw the Snake, pretty much as you see it from your source, minus the head and tail.

Snake-to-Dragon Transformation...

First I have drawn the Snake pretty much as before, only without his head or tail because those will change.

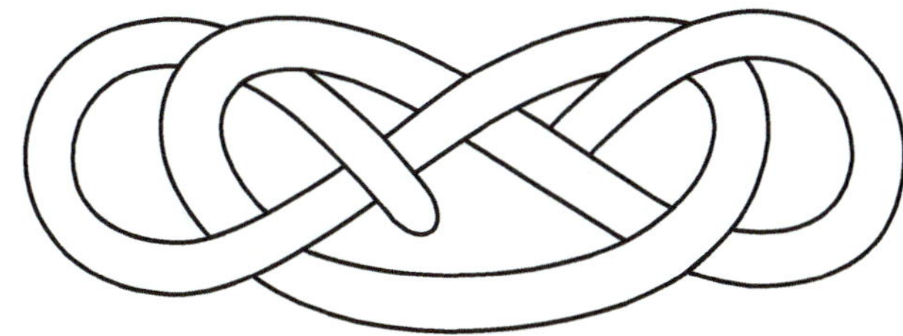

Then a portion of the body has been erased where the head will go, and I have started the head shape of my Dragon. You can invent any style of head for the Dragon that you want, but I will show you how to do the one that I like to use for my Dragons. Begin with a sloping line that starts where the old Snake head used to emerge from the knot. The two big bumps that you see in the example will form the eyebrow and the nose, and they can be made as pronounced as you like. Keep in mind that the head can be tweaked after it's made, so it doesn't have to be perfect at this point.

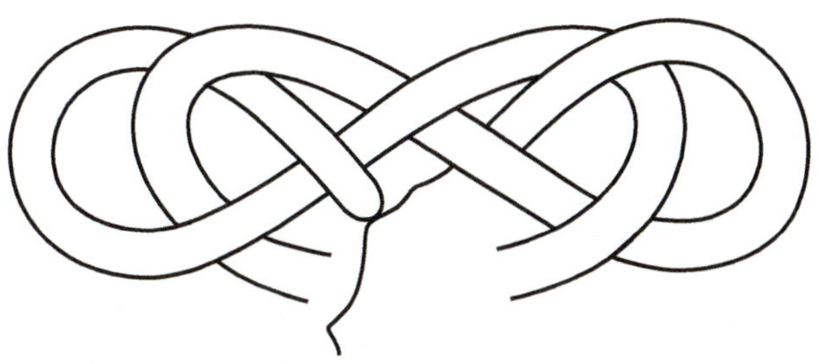

Now I finish the other half of the head. Starting at the throat I swoop out to make the cheek. This swoops in again to make a small mouth and muzzle area, before joining up to the nose made before.

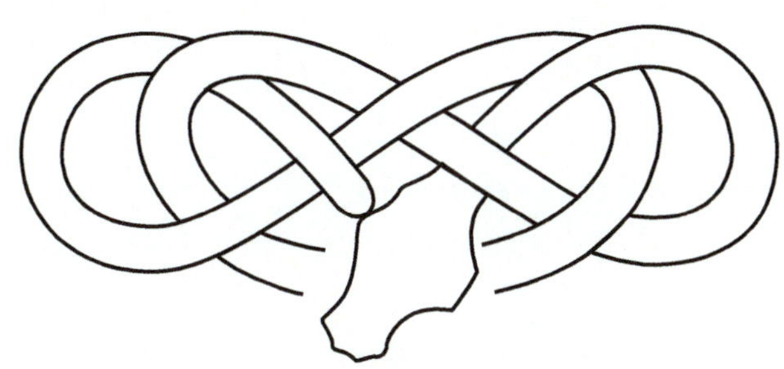

Snake-to-Dragon Transformation...

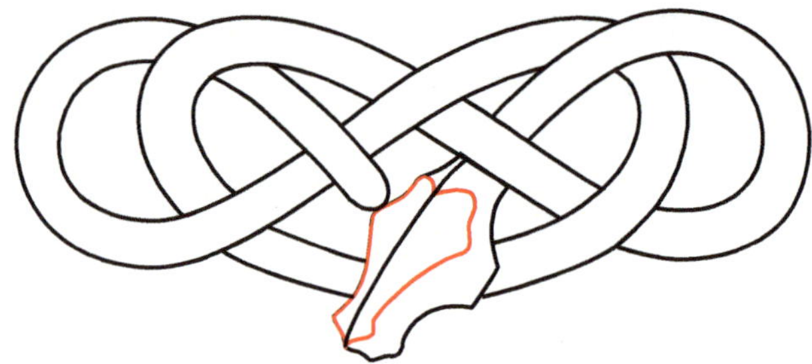

I also like to put a brow-plate on some of my Dragons, so I'll show you how to do that next. Start by drawing a center line from not quite the middle of the back of his head and then continue down until you reach the point of his nose. The brow-plates branch out from this center line. To make the brow-plate on the side of his head facing us, make a line that basically mirrors that outside edge of his face, then simply join that to the outside of his head to make the other side.

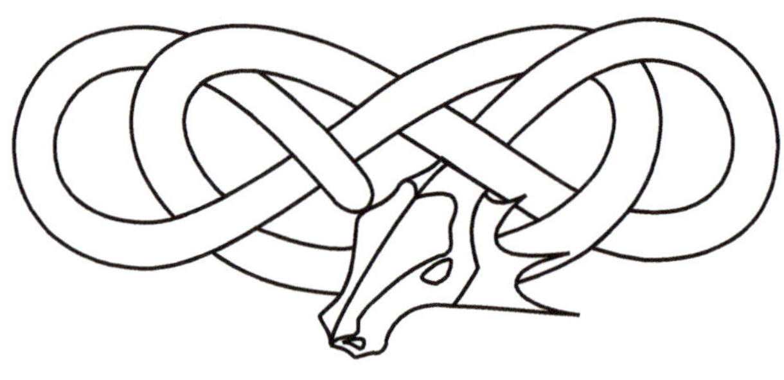

I'm going to add a decorative fan coming from his cheek to give him a water serpent look. This is a swooping line that starts from his throat and then eventually ends at his cheekbone. Make this as swooped as you want. To finish, I add his eye below the brow-plate and a nostril to his nose.

Snake-to-Dragon Transformation...

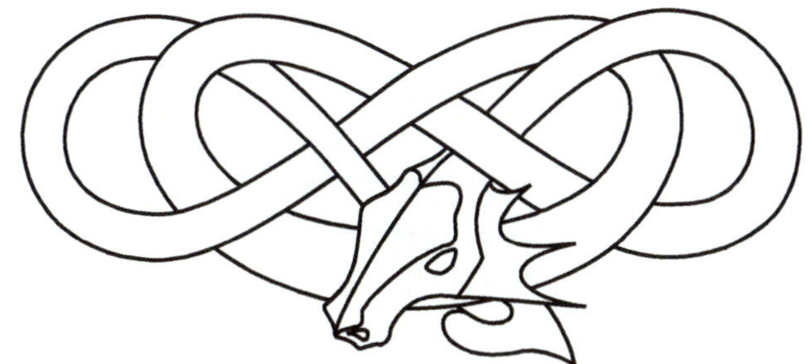

Snakes are generally pretty skinny from start to finish, so for my Dragons I like to add some curves to the body. The knot should remain pretty symmetrical, so the place I have picked for my "belly bulge" is the curve that his head passes over, on the bottom of the knot. His body will taper to either side of this bulge, only slightly toward his head and then much more pronounced toward his tail. I have also elongated the tail here so that it crosses under his head. I've ended the tail with a heart shape for fun.

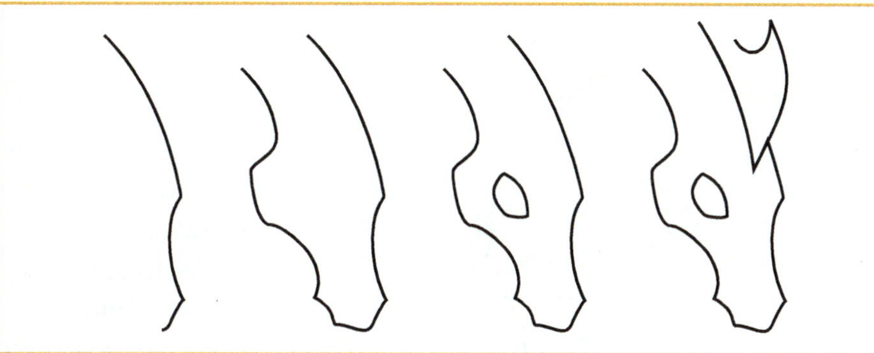

Here's how to draw a simple Dragon head. First draw the top of his head. It has one bend in it, which will become his eyebrow, and then swoops down to curve around where his nose will be.

To draw the lower half of the face, start at the throat and jut out to round out his jaw or cheekbone, then swoop in to the muzzle area to join with the nose.

All there is left to add is the eye. On this version I've also added a head crest to spiff him up a bit. This is how I draw my Dragons, but try some ideas from other cultures like Chinese or Aztec, or the Medieval era. Don't be afraid to create new themes and styles for your Dragons.

Turning a Knot into a Dragon

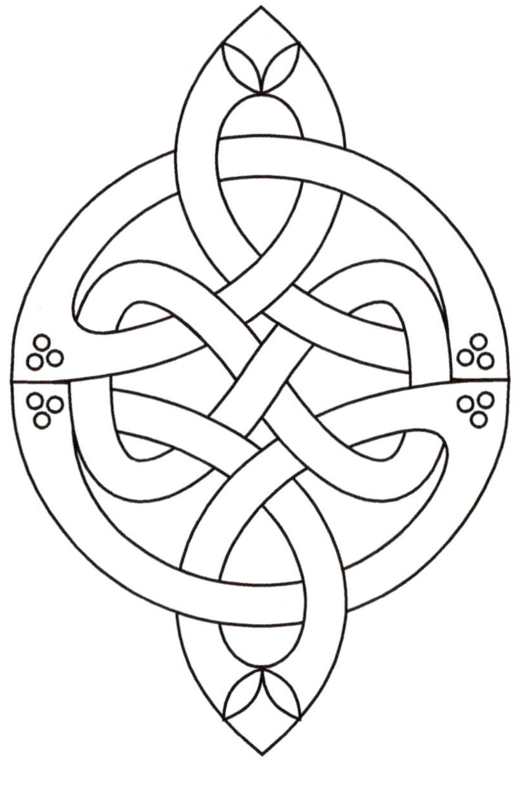

Here we have a little knot that I created. To turn this into a Dragon, find a place in the knot that makes the most sense visually to "break" the knotwork pattern. The break is where the head and tail will meet when it becomes a Dragon. In this example, I've chosen to make my break at the top of this particular knot. I think the top will show off the little dragon-to-be better than if I had broken it at the bottom, side, or middle.

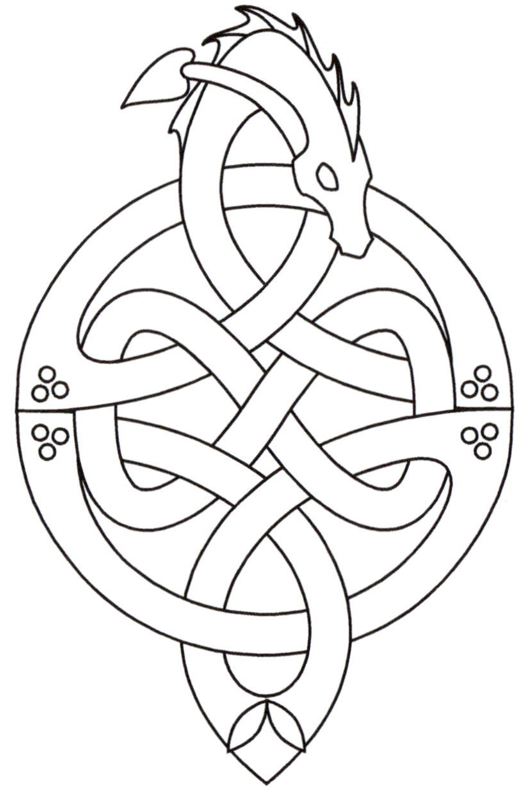

Here you can see the knot with the Dragon head added, and his tail brought up and around under his chin. The knot or body of the Dragon was tapered where it came to the tail, as in the Snake-into-a-Dragon section. On this Dragon I have also added a crest, which is of course optional. Because the knot I chose was fairly thick, there wasn't a whole lot of work to make it into a Dragon. A really thin knotwork design might have required making the body thicker in the Dragon's middle again to give him that "belly bulge," but he looks okay as he is here so I'll leave it.

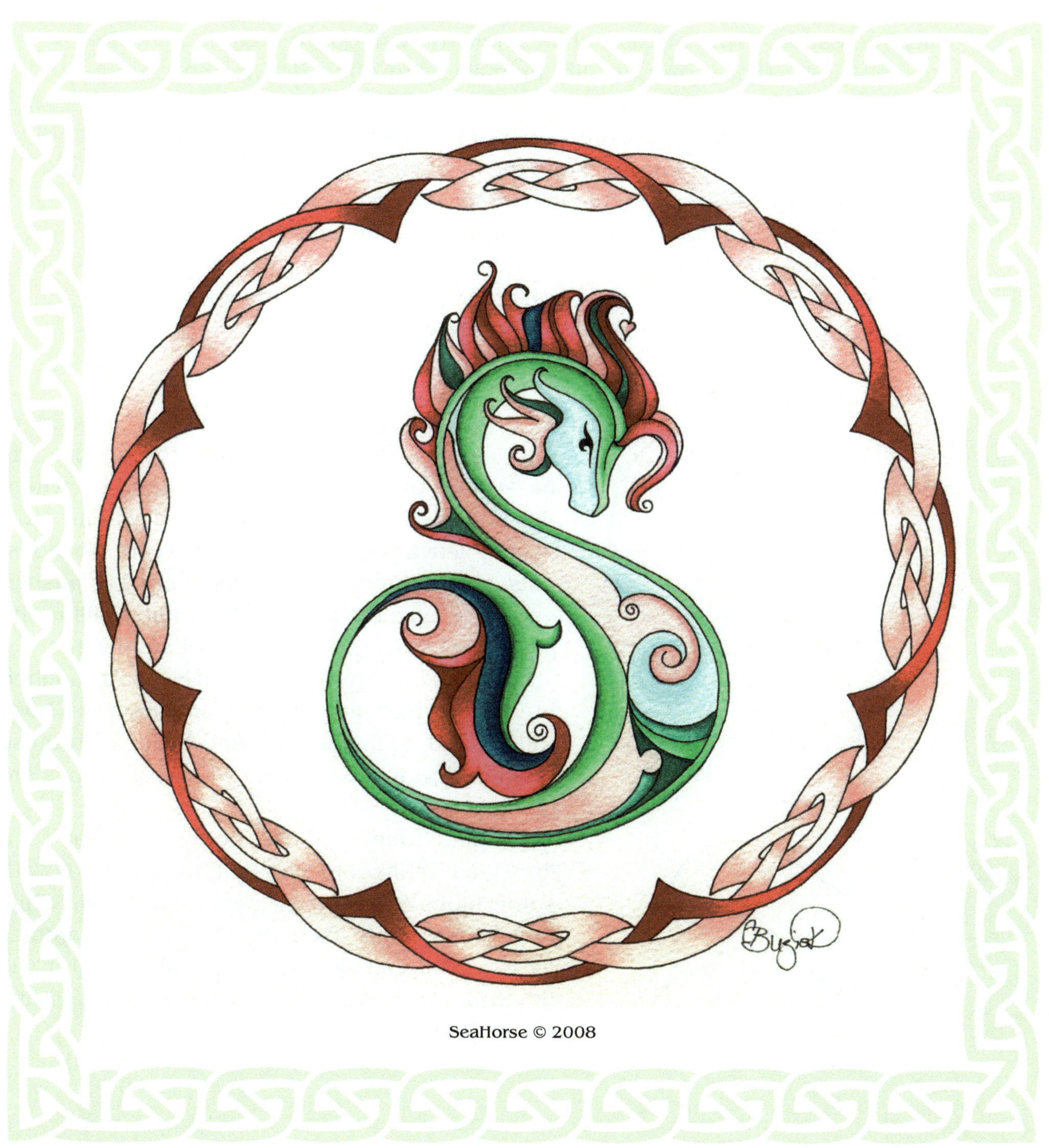

SeaHorse © 2008

Celtic Animals

Animals were all around the ancient Celts—used for food, labor, status, and "recreation." Who needs Netflix when you can go on a cattle raid! So it's no wonder that in ancient life animals were often drawn and carved on anything from jewelry to stone to parchment. The Celts took it one step further. They didn't just draw their animals sitting there; they twisted, wrapped, tangled, and bent them into the most crazy and amazing positions! While there may not have been many two-legged dogs with 10-foot-long tails to use as a model to draw from, the really great Celtic animals can be easily recognized for what they must have been referenced from in real life. So if you're having trouble, find a photo of a real animal and examine it for clues of what may be wrong or needed in your drawing.

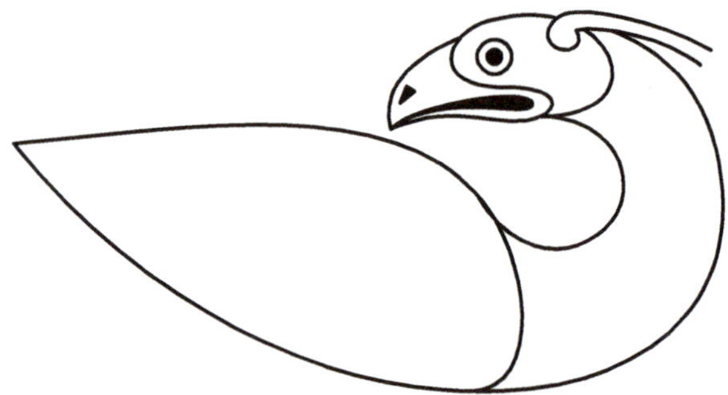

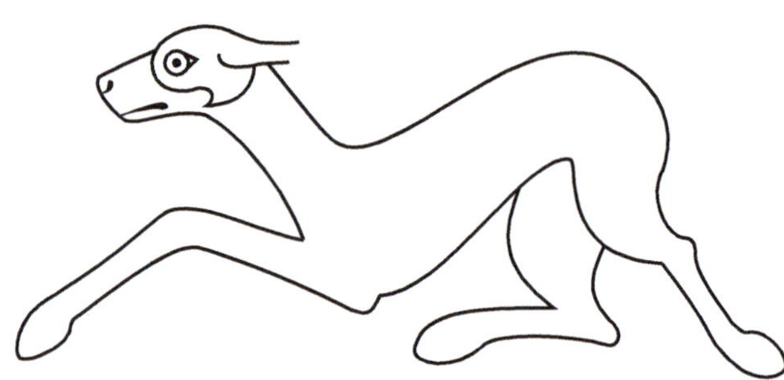

To start, I usually draw a "blob" version of my animal to block out where the shapes will be—where the head will bend around to, where the body lies, and where the legs will end up. I usually leave the drawing of the ears, tongues, tails, and feathers until the main body is finished and then I use the various extra bits to fill in the gaps, depending on what type of animal it is.

For example, to the left I have a bird roughed in, using a teardrop to block in where his body will be and adding a neck and head. With these roughed in I know where my general shapes are going to be.

For the hound (whose body is similar to a lion's, as we'll see) I block in a rough body with some blobs for his legs, neck, and head. While I've added some face details in my examples here so you can see what kind of animal it will be, you can leave yours even rougher if that's easier for you.

The Celtic Hound

The best examples to use when drawing a Celtic Hound are Irish Wolfhounds. One look at their shaggy faces and tall bodies and you'll know exactly what the Celts were drawing from when making their Celtic hounds!

Drawing the Face

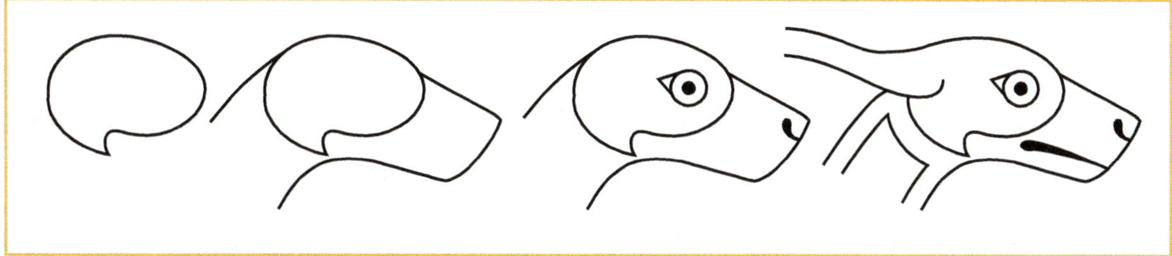

To draw the head of the Hound, start with an oval shape with a little tail on the bottom of one corner. It should look almost like a speech balloon from a comic book.

Next add your muzzle shape, which should come off the oval nearly level with the top. The muzzle can taper a bit at the nose if you like. The muzzle piece curves down and around and eventually becomes his neck/throat. Now add the back of the neck to the head of the Hound.

Add the eye and nose markings. Scoop the ear out from the oval shape, near the top. The mouth is added in the muzzle area and the inner outline is added to the neck, where it would continue down through the body.

You can also draw the Hound with an open mouth and teeth, or have him biting on something, like his own body, a leg, or even another animal. You can also leave his mouth open and have his tongue extending out, and then you can weave his tongue too!

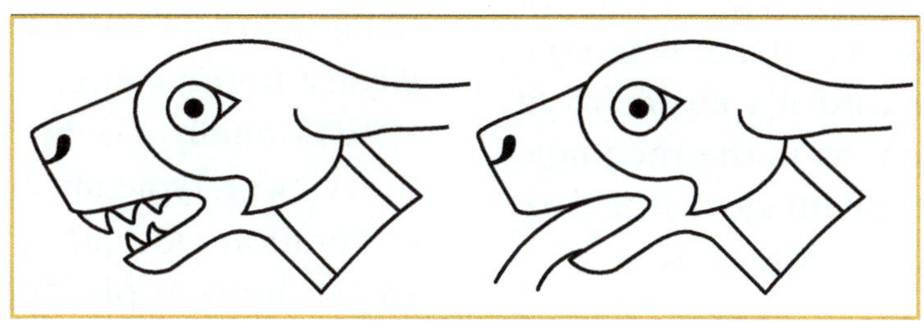

The Celtic hound...

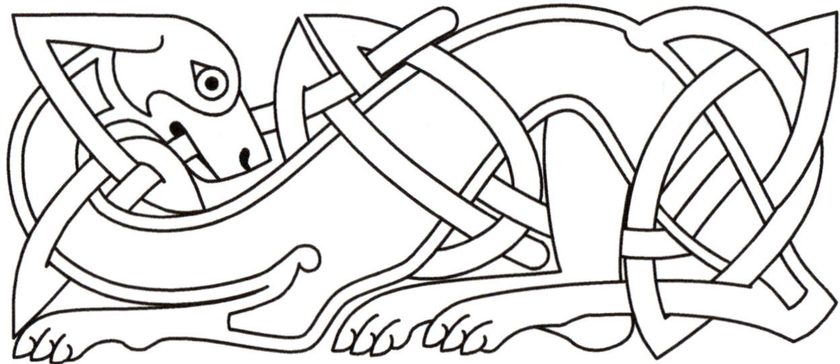

The Body

Celtic Hounds are modeled after the Irish Wolfhound so you can use images of those as a guide so far as general anatomy goes. Our Celtic Hounds, however, will be much more bent out of shape!

The body is drawn with a double outline or border as shown above. This border usually ends on the legs at about the elbow/knee point and the neck, where it is shown either as a blunt or rounded end. The border is not usually drawn on the leg farthest from the viewer, but it can be if you want.

The Head

The head is usually shown looking back over the body, although facing forward or backward is acceptable. I find that when the Hound is facing backward it's easier to fit him into a shaped area, as in the rectangle I made him fit here. If the image is freeform on the page, he can face either way.

The Legs

The legs in the front and back should be drawn bent, with hip/shoulder, knee/elbow, and ankle/wrist joints. Due to the ways you have to contort the Hound to make him fit into a particular shape, sometimes not all the joints are used or more joints are added. For very complex designs involving Hounds the bends don't even have to make sense—his leg can end up bending backward, for example.

Usually two of each leg are shown, but it's all right to have only one of each or one front leg and two back legs. Depending on the space you have to fit the Hound into, decide which is best for your picture. One back leg and two front legs is hardly ever done and looks a little odd. The back leg that's farthest from the viewer is always stretched forward of the other leg, as shown on the previous page. If a back leg needs to be extended behind the animal, it is always the leg that is closest to the viewer.

Additionally, only the leg closest to the viewer typically has decoration on it. Decoration can either be parallel bands as shown here, triple dots on the hip, or two bands of color separated by a patterned design, such as knots or maze patterns.

Toes are drawn in either threes or twos, and you should try to have the same number of toes on the front and back feet of your Hound.

Extended Bits

In the case of the Hound, the tail and ears are extended and knotted. The neck is often elongated as well, and so are the legs, but usually not to the complex extent of the tail and ears. The Hound is often depicted as biting something, so if you can get a piece of tail or his ear to wrap around for him to bite it's a good idea. He can also be drawn as if he's biting other animals or his own legs or body.

The extended bits on the Hound should follow the same weaving pattern as a regular knot, going over and under his legs, body, and other extended bits. A few liberties can be taken when doing this; for example, you always want his face to be seen, so you can ignore the over and under rule when you go past his head if you have to.

Generally only one ear is drawn.

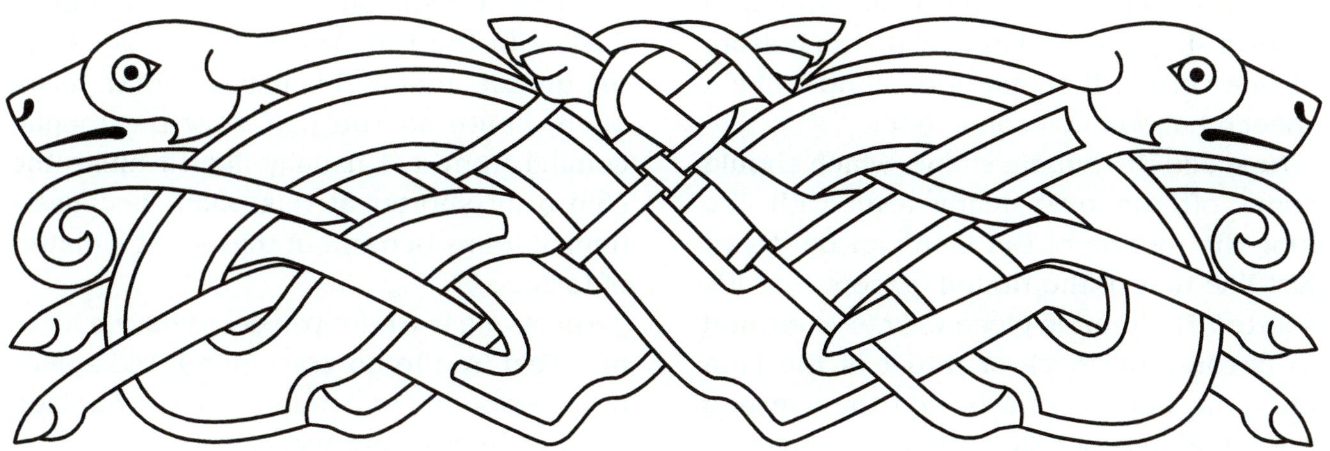

The Celtic Lion

The nice thing about the Celtic Lion is that he's started almost the exact same way as the Hound. He also shares many body features of the Hound, so once you've mastered one image you should be able to draw the other with ease.

Drawing the Face

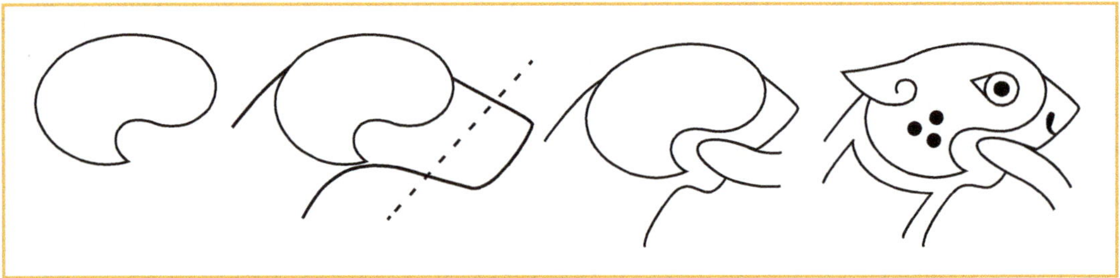

To draw the head of the Lion, start with an oval shape with a little tail on the bottom of one corner. It should look almost like a speech balloon in a comic book.

Next add the muzzle shape, which should come off the oval nearly level with the top. The muzzle of the Lion can be drawn just like that of the Hound, except that it's shorter. The muzzle piece will curve around to become the neck or throat of the Lion once the body is drawn. Add the eye and nose markings. Whisker marks are drawn as triple dots on his cheek.

Scoop the ear out from the oval shape, flush with the top. The mouth is added in the muzzle area and is usually drawn as an open mouth so you can draw the tongue coming from it. I usually like to make the chin a bit shorter at this point, because I think it looks better, but that's just a matter of taste.

The mane is where you get to have a lot of fun. Feel free to go crazy here! Add spikes or waves or mix and match to give your Lion personality and interest.

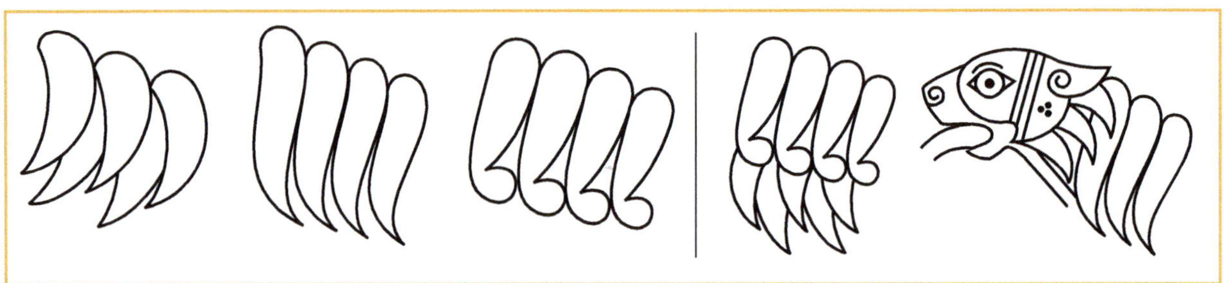

The Celtic Lion...

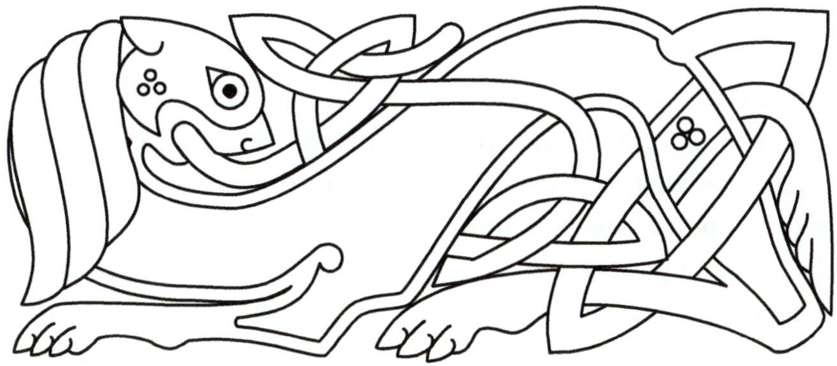

The Body

The body of the Celtic Lion is very similar to that of the Celtic Hound. The body is drawn with a double outline or border as shown above. This border usually ends on the legs at about the elbow/knee point and the neck, where it is shown either as a blunt or rounded end. The border is not usually drawn on the leg farthest from the viewer (if that rear leg is drawn at all).

The Head

The head is usually depicted as looking back over the body, although facing forward or backward is acceptable. If the image is freeform on the page then the Lion can face either way.

The mane usually is drawn covering the whole neck of the Lion. In the old manuscripts you can always tell if it's a Lion as opposed to a Hound by the mane and the shorter muzzle. The Lion usually has three little dots on the cheek as whiskers or sometimes stripes in the cheek and dots as well. The tongue is almost always drawn.

The Legs

The legs in the front and back bend, with hip/shoulder, knee/elbow, and ankle/wrist joints. As with the Hound, due to the ways you may have to contort the Lion to make him fit a particular shape, sometimes not all the joints are used or more joints are added.

Again, as with the Hound, usually two of each leg are shown but it's all right to have only one of each or one front leg and two back legs. Showing one back leg and two front legs is hardly ever done. The back leg that is farthest from the viewer is always stretched forward of the other leg, as shown in the illustration. If a back leg needs to be extended behind the animal, it is always the leg that is closest to the viewer.

Only the leg closest to the viewer is ever decorated. Decoration can either be triple dots, colored bands, or two bands of color bordering a patterned design, such as knots, maze patterns, or triple dots, as shown in the illustration.

Toes are drawn in either threes or twos, with the same number of toes on the front and back feet of your Lion.

The Celtic Lion...

Extended Bits

In the case of the Lion, the tail and tongue are extended and knotted. The neck and the legs are often elongated as well, but usually not to the complex extent of the tail and tongue. The Lion is often depicted with his tongue lolling out and knotted around his body.

The extended bits on the Lion should weave like a regular knot, going over and under legs, body, and other extended bits.

His tail is usually drawn with a decorative tuft of some sort on the end, usually something to match the style of the mane. There are a lot of different historical examples of tail ends in ancient manuscripts to refer to, or feel free to develop your own tail and make it as decorative as you want or need.

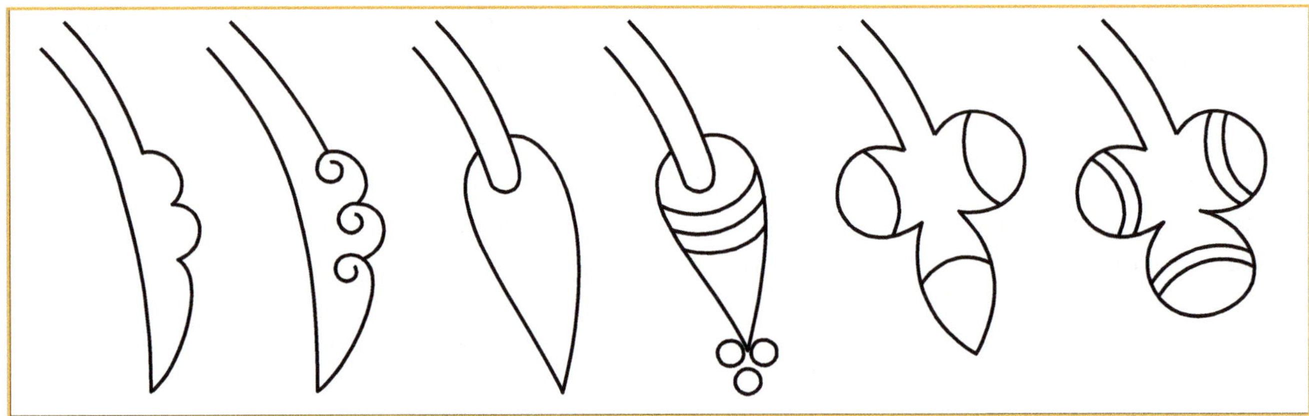

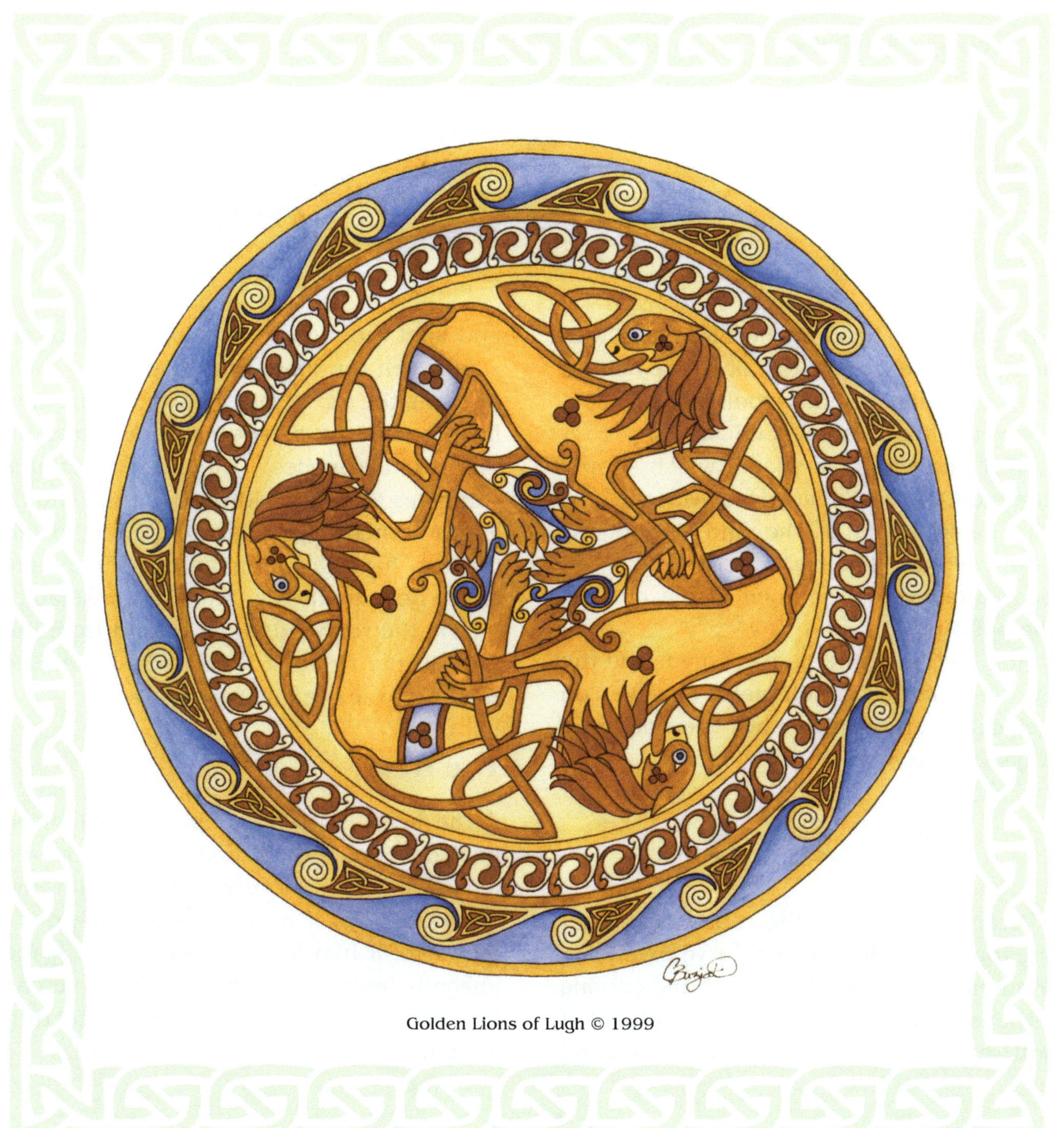

Golden Lions of Lugh © 1999

The Celtic Bird

Drawing the Face

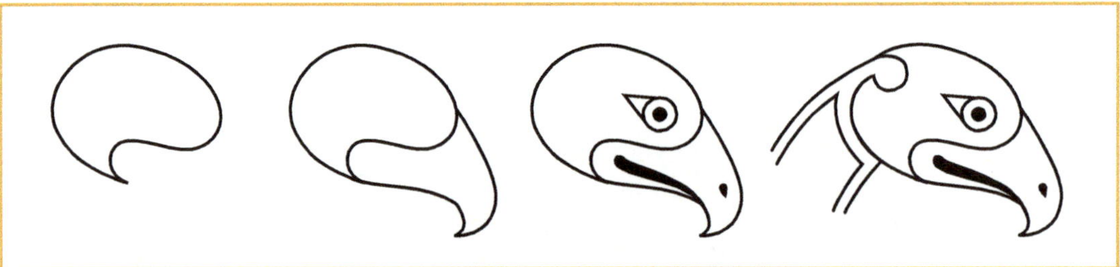

To draw the head of the Bird, start with an oval shape with a little tail on the bottom of one corner. It should look almost like a speech balloon from a comic book.

Next add the beak shape, which should come off the oval nearly level with the top. The beak tapers at the end and hooks down slightly, like an eagle's beak. The beak attaches to the point of the oval on the bottom.

Add the mouth in the beak area. Add the eye and the nostril hole next. The eyes on Celtic animals may be drawn a few different ways, as shown here:

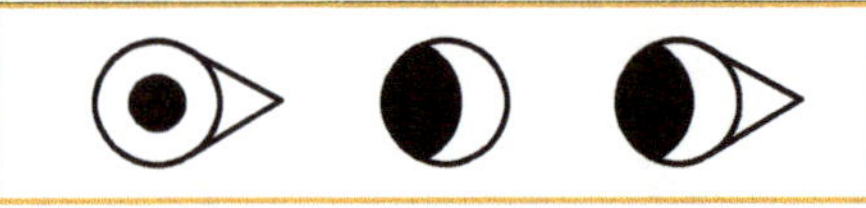

Attach the neck to the oval shape, near the top. The little rounded curve extending from the back of the Bird's neck and curving into his head is how the head would look if you weren't going to make an "ear" to extend and knot around the drawing. The "ear" is what I call the long, thin strand that trails out from the top of the birds' heads in some images (see the finished bird examples on the next two pages). There are traditional examples with and without it, so the choice is yours whether you want to draw it. To add the ear, have the rounded curve continue out to become the ear knotwork, instead of having the rounded curve extend from the back of the neck into the bird's head. See the Bird example on the next page.

The Head

The head is usually depicted as looking back over the body, although facing forward or backward is acceptable. As with the other animals, if he's facing backward it's easier to fit him into a shaped area. If the image is freeform on the page then he can face either way, but with the Birds I feel they look more attractive facing backward.

The Celtic Bird...

The Body

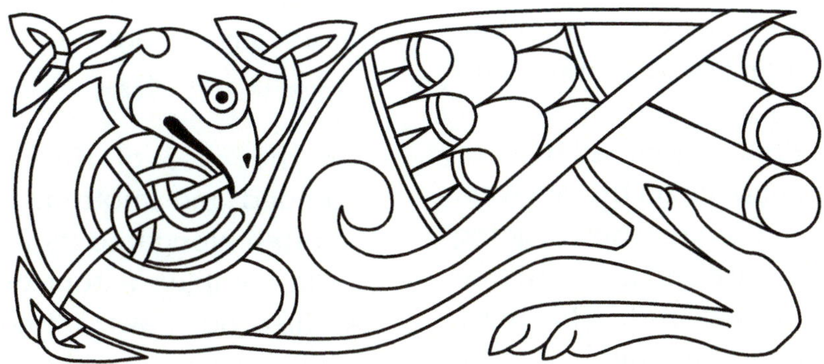

Celtic Birds were usually peacocks, doves, or eagles. I think peacocks were the most common, which might explain the decorative tails and bright colors and designs on many of them.

The body is drawn with the double outline or border as shown above. This border usually ends high up on the legs, near where they attach to the body, and on the neck below the face.

The wing is a teardrop shape, with the lower portion edged by a curling spiral-type design that starts on his shoulder and continues out to the point of the teardrop.

The wing feathers can either cover the entire wing or just appear as a band on it, as shown above. The feathers themselves can be decorated as the first row are in my wing above, or can be plain like the rest of the ones in the wing band.

Tail feathers come out of the bottom of the wing, between the teardrop point and the leg(s). Tail feathers usually have little disks drawn on the ends.

Feathers

Designing feathers in the tail and wings are the best part of drawing Birds! Feel free to go crazy here—add any kind of details you can think of for style and decoration.

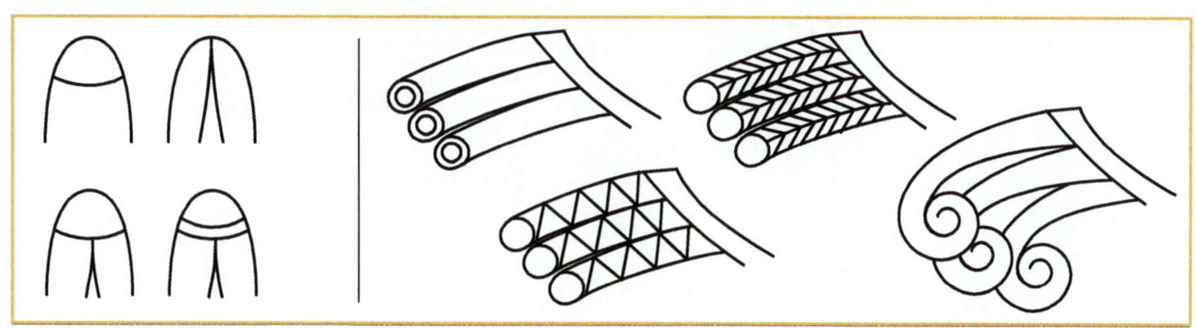

The Celtic Bird...

The Legs

The legs on the Bird usually have only the knee and hip joint; then the toes branch off at the end.

The toes can be drawn in either twos or threes and can be bent back on themselves. Usually one or two toes are shown going toward the front of the bird and the third one is bent back (as on a real bird). The bent-back one can be on the horizontal, like the front two, or even bent up at a 90-degree angle if necessary—whatever you need to make it fit in the area.

Either one or both legs are usually shown. Draw two if they fit or only one if they don't. The leg that is farthest from the viewer is always stretched forward. If a leg needs to be extended behind the animal, it is always the leg that is closest to the viewer. Legs are not usually decorated.

Extended Bits

In the case of the Bird, the ears are extended and knotted. The neck and toes are often elongated as well, but usually not to the complex extent of the ear. The Bird can also be drawn biting something, such as his ear, wing, or another animal.

The extended bits on the Bird should weave like a regular knot, going over and under his legs, body, toes, and other extended bits. Again, a few liberties can be taken when doing this; for example, you always want his face to show, so ignore the over and under rule when going past his head.

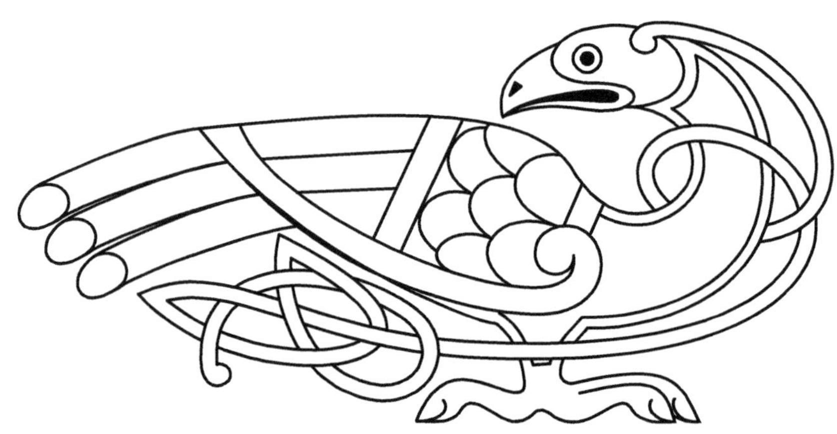

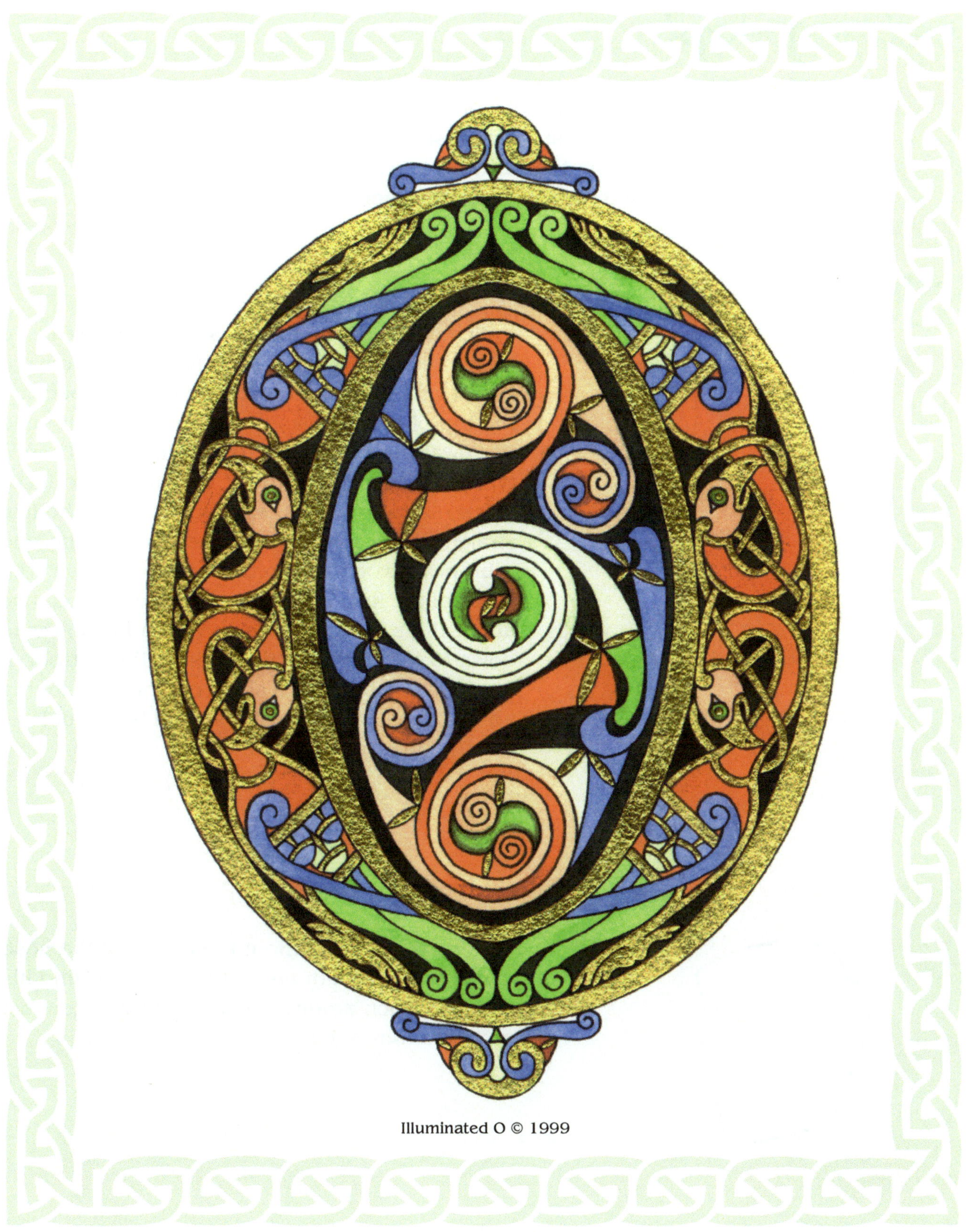

Illuminated O © 1999

Celtic People

Celtic People are a common type of decoration in Celtic manuscripts, usually found tangled up in strange positions and colorfully decorated. While it may sound daunting to draw People, the unique Celtic style of art makes it easier than you'd think to include People in your artwork!

Celtic Man

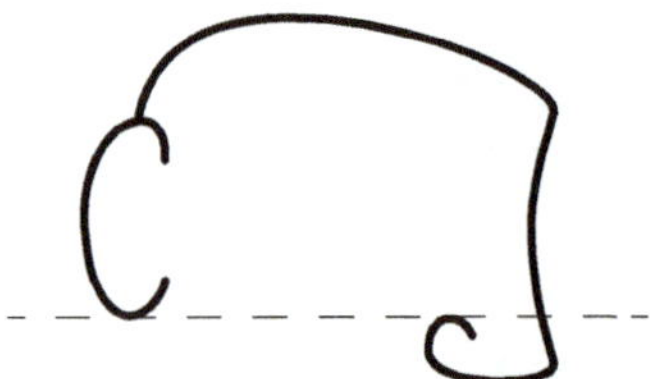

First we'll begin with a close-up of the head. To start, draw a "C" shape for the Man's ear. From the top of that make a curved line that will become the top of his head and his forehead, then bend downward to begin the front of his face. There's typically not a whole lot of curving in the faces when drawn in profile, so you can bring the line straight down from the forehead or maybe add a bit of a swoop out to the tip of the nose. The width of the head from ear to forehead should be about the same as the length from his forehead down to the tip of his nose. Bring the bottom of his nose in a bit, with a small curl or hook for the nostril. Typically the nostril should be about level with the bottom of his ear.

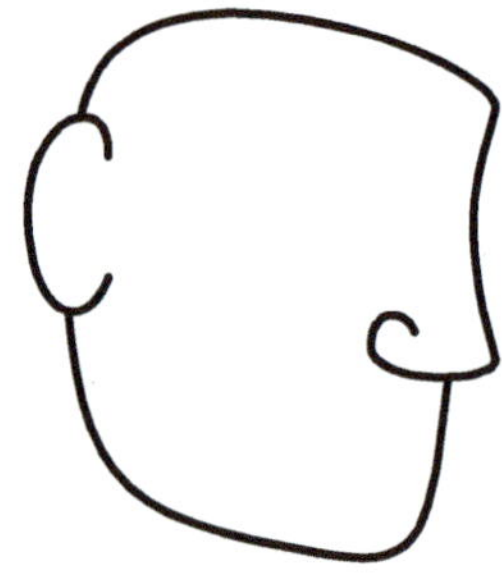

Come down from about the center of the nose to create the mouth area, then curve around his chin and back around his jaw until you connect to the bottom of his ear.

Celtic people...

Draw a "V" shape to mark off the top line of his beard, connecting from the front part of his lower ear to his nostril. I've also added his hair (we'll cover more examples of hair later). The hair attaches to the top of his forehead and follows the shape of his head, attaching again to the back of his neck.

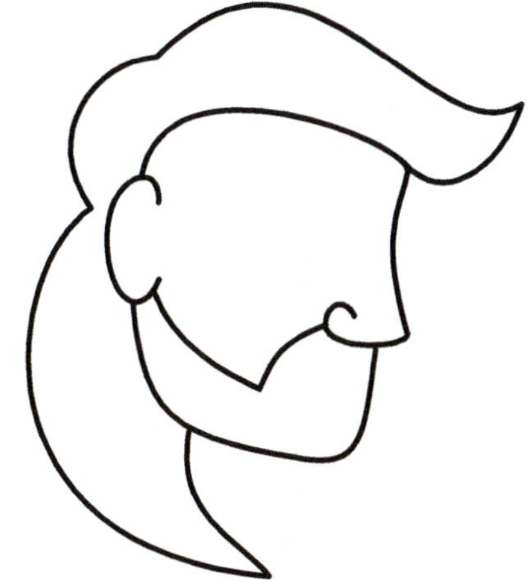

Add a few more facial features next, such as a curve for the eyebrow and a mouth. His eye is drawn rather like an almond shape, with a circle for the iris in the center and a pupil inside that. I've also started to draw his beard from his chin, as indicated by the dashed lines. Weaving his beard can be done or not, but usually it is done. You can weave up the beard after the man is finished.

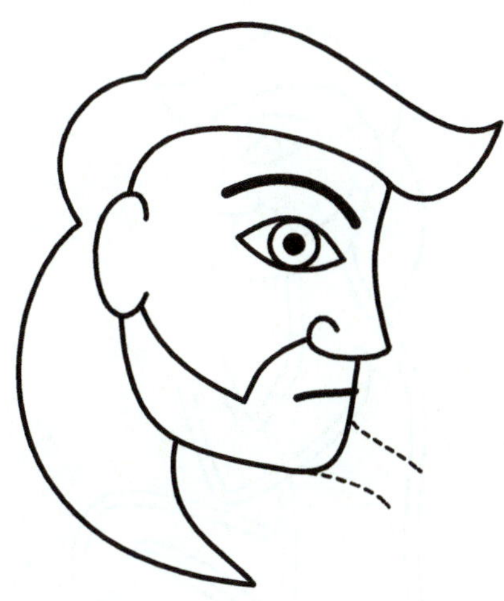

Celtic people...

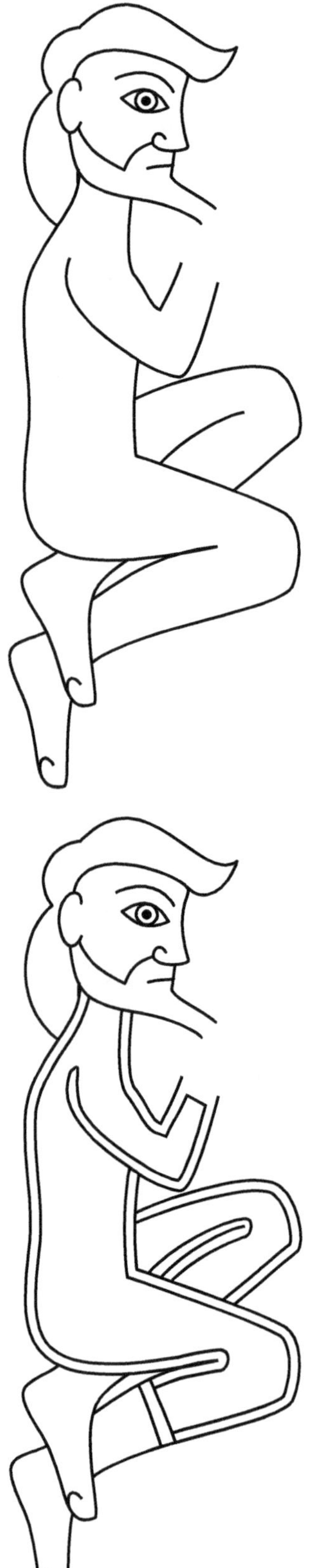

Now that the head is finished, focus on the rest of the Man's body. From the back of his neck, continue down his back and then curve around his rear. On his front, draw down his chest a little way and then bend out for an arm, which I've drawn in the example as bent at the elbow. We'll deal with the hand in a little bit. From below his arm, draw down past his belly and then make his hip and the rest of his front leg. His other leg I am going to draw in the background. While People are drawn usually with both legs, you can have one arm or two, depending on the room you have. The more you can add the better, as it will create more places we can knot up later. His feet are drawn almost like two little triangles. Note that his toes are nothing more than a little curl on the underside of each foot.

To add more detail, add another line along the inside of his body. Start under his head and end at his calf with another double line, rather like a cuff or band. His wrist should also have a cuff.

Celtic people...

The next step is to add a hand, which I'm showing here as a clenched fist to hold onto his beard. I've also added a pair of bands above and below his waist and another one on his thigh. These bands serve as dividers when you color your Person, and each section can be a different color. Ankles are drawn as small circles on the feet. When colored, the ankles are traditionally a red outlined circle or a red-filled dot.

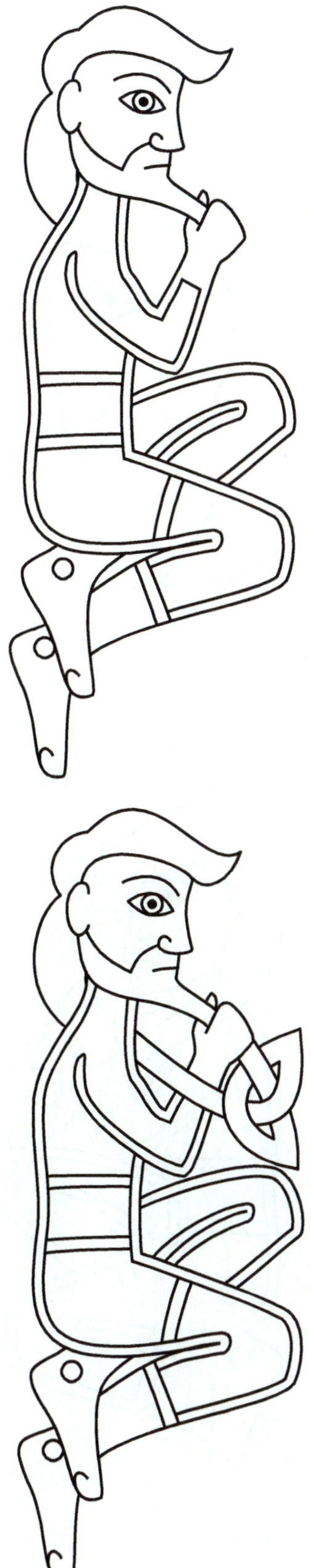

Finally, I complete his beard. The beard continues from his hand where he's holding it, makes a small knot, then eventually joins up with his hair behind his neck. This lock of hair can join up with the beard over the front of his neck or behind, depending on what is required from the overs and unders of the knot part. I've shown here a rather simple knot, but the knot can also be tangled up and around the Person, even through his legs and around his body as much as you like. Make sure to keep the overs and unders correct as much as possible, so that the beard passes over and under as it weaves through his body parts and through other pieces of the knot.

Celtic people...

Celtic Woman

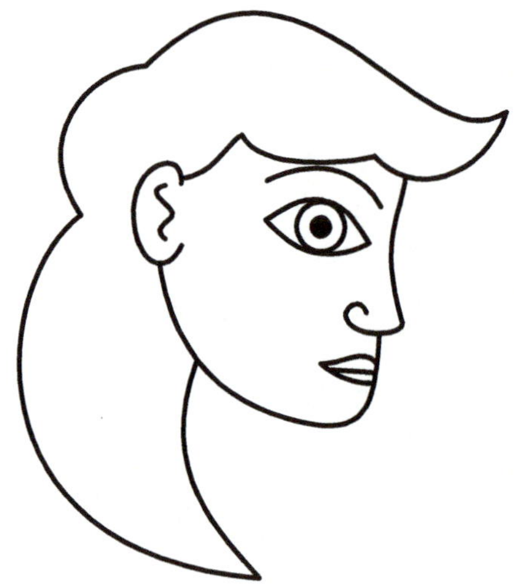

To make the Celtic Woman we begin with a Celtic Man's head, but alter it to make it more feminine. Here I've begun with the same shapes used for the Man, but have made the eyebrow thinner, the chin and jaw smaller, and the eye larger. I've also shortened the nose a bit. Drawings of Celtic Women didn't usually show earrings; however, if you want to add one a round circle would match. Necklaces, torcs, rings, and arm bands were worn by both sexes of the Celts so these could easily be added as well.

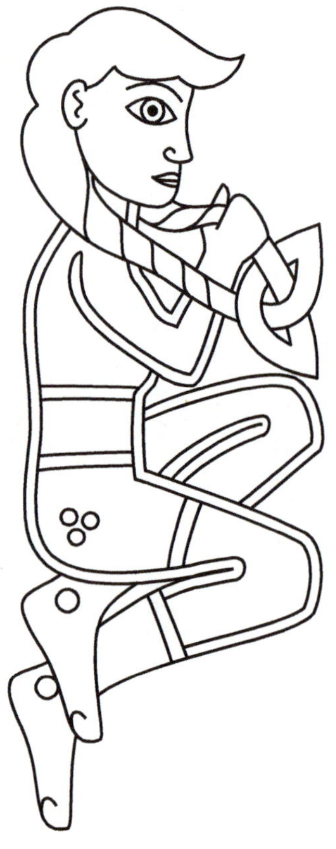

To make the Celtic Woman's figure a little more ladylike, I've made her chest curve out where it joins under her arm to imply a bust. Because she doesn't have a beard, I've given her braids on the sides of her head to make a knot with. The braids are drawn very simply here, with just a twist added to the locks on either side where they leave her head. You'll notice that I did a "no-no" here by not weaving the braid closest to the viewer through her arm and neck (it passes over both, making an over-over in the pattern), but I felt that was a small sacrifice in order to be able to see the braid better.

Celtic people...

Hairstyles & Beards

You can mix and match among these many variations of hairstyles or make up your own. The Man in the tutorial has plain or wavy hair, but there are many other styles shown in the Book of Kells which I'll go through here.

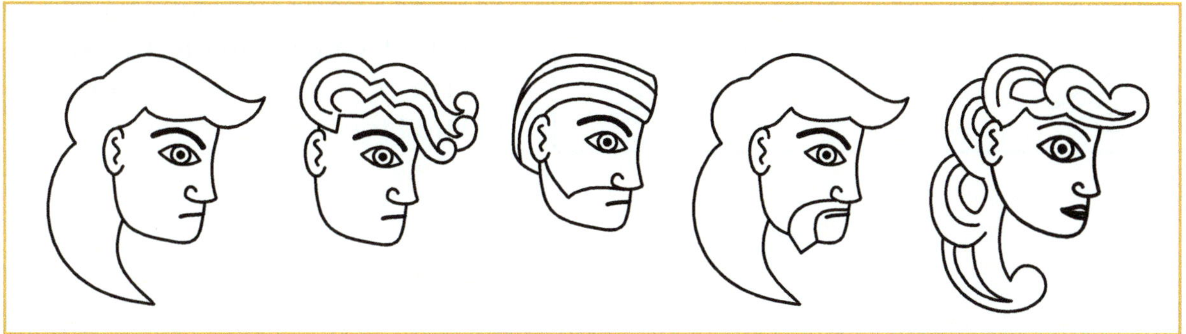

The first Man here sports wavy hair. There are small "bumps" added around the hair to give the impression of more body, and the bangs have been drawn out and curled up. These could also be extended to become woven knotwork, and maybe attached to his beard or another lock of hair.

The second Man has spiky, curly hair. There are a few "bumps" around it and the curly bangs as well. Some interior angular lines have been added within the hair to imply spiky waves. Although nothing in this current hairstyle is woven, you could add a matching ponytail to him if you wanted some hair to weave up after.

The third Man has short, slicked-back hair. He also sports a simple, smooth beard.

The fourth Man has a great handlebar mustache. The ends of this could be left finished like this, they could be curled into rounded nubs like the second Man's bangs, or even pulled out into a long strand that could be knotted.

Our lovely lady in the last example is drawn with quite curly hair. The "bumps" are more defined and are outlined again inside the hair, giving the impression of even more curls.

Any of these hairstyles could be used or mixed and matched for Men or Women. Don't be afraid to add long hair to your Men, either!

ZOOMORPHICS

Celtic people...

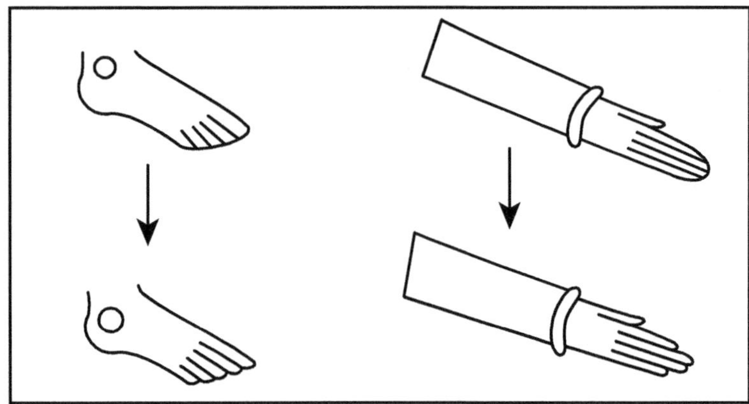

The examples to the left show an easy method for drawing feet and hands, but you can also fully draw them out. Try making the hand into a "mitten" shape and then just add in the fingers as lines. To make it more realistic, you can add curves to define each fingertip. The foot can be made the same way, with a rounded "slipper" end or with defined toes.

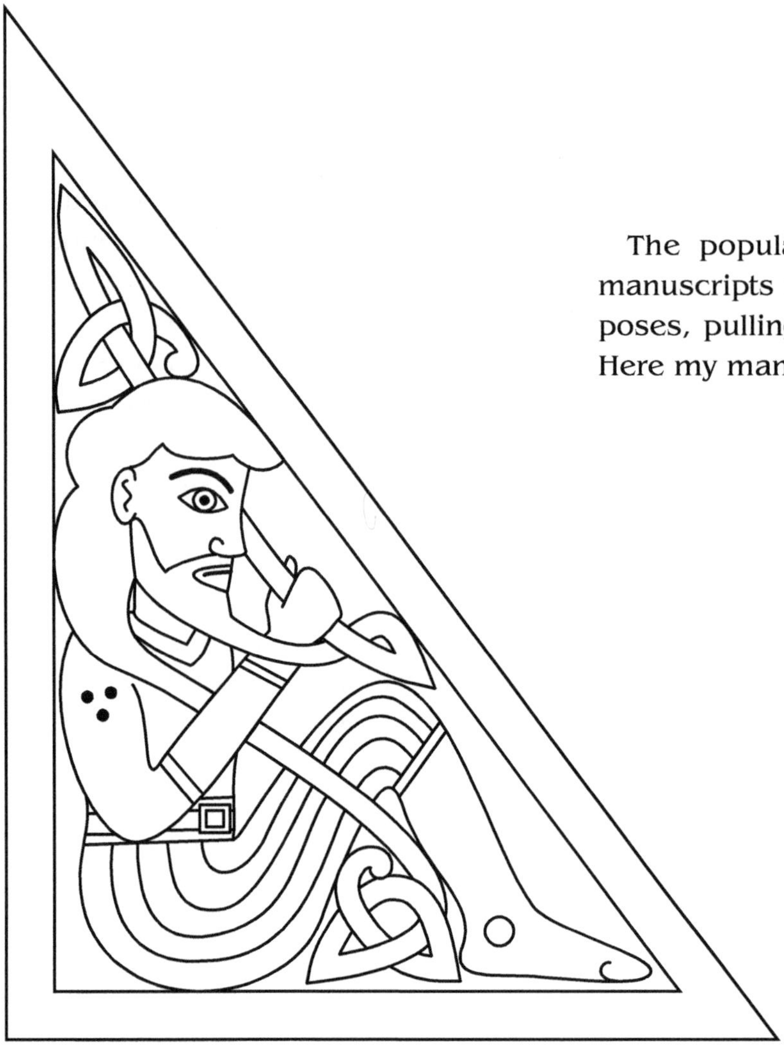

The popular "Beard Puller" images in Celtic manuscripts feature a man or men tangled up in poses, pulling their own or each other's beards. Here my man has striped trousers and a belt.

Vine & Chalice

The natural world was an important part of daily life for any ancient culture, and the Celts were no exception. Plants and animals were part of a typical Celtic person's daily routine, and the natural world was also responsible for the forces creating chaos and catastrophe as well as food and sustenance.

Although the Vine & Chalice motif may typically be considered a "Christian-era" design, its usage dates back further in stone and metal works. The classical "palmette," "lotus," and "lyre" shapes can be seen in early Celtic design, as well as in Coptic and Greek art.

The chalice shape is very easy to draw—essentially it's an hourglass. The sides of the hourglass are curved to mimic the sides of a cup. The cup is traditionally drawn with the top and bottom halves in equal proportion as shown on the left, or the top can be accented as you see on the right.

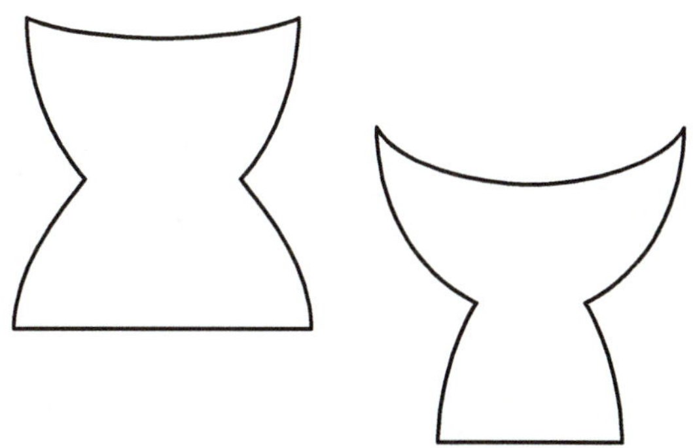

The chalice can be decorated in the usual Celtic manner, with an extra outline or piping around it. It's also acceptable to add some stripes at the mouth of the cup, like a rim or decorative band at the top. The common Celtic triple dot motif can be added for interest. Some suppose that the triple dots represent berries in Celtic art, so maybe it's especially appropriate to have grape berries on the wine chalices.

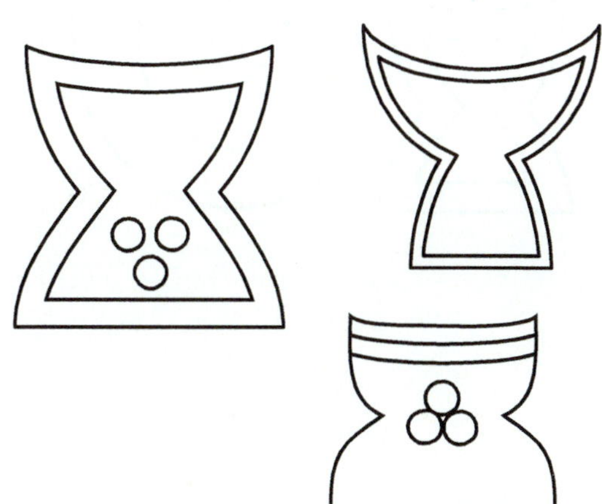

Vine & Chalice...

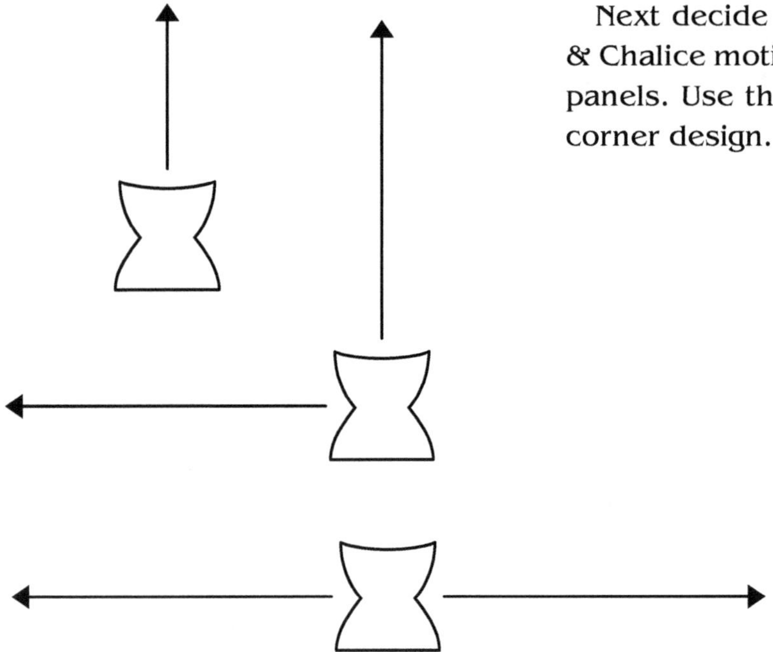

Next decide on the overall design shape. Vine & Chalice motifs are excellent for using as border panels. Use them horizontally, vertically, or as a corner design.

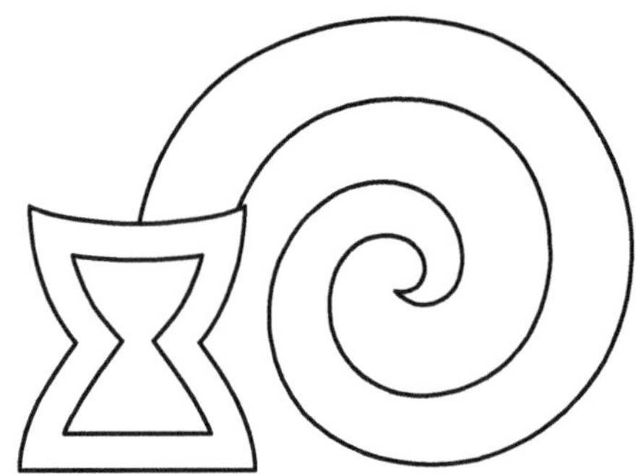

Let's begin with a horizontal design. I'll only work on half of the design at a time so there is more room to work, and then we'll duplicate our final vines on the other side of the chalice when we've finished.

Begin with the chalice. From the right half of the chalice mouth draw a curling tendril of vine. The vine makes a full curl, with enough space so the sides don't touch each other. This space will be used later on to weave in leaves, so allow yourself some room for these additions. Also notice how the vine curl appears slightly tapered, so the tip is slimmer than the base that emerges from the chalice.

Vine & Chalice...

Subsequent curls are easy to add—just spring one off of the next in the opposite direction! Notice how the curls at the top and bottom remain in line with each other.

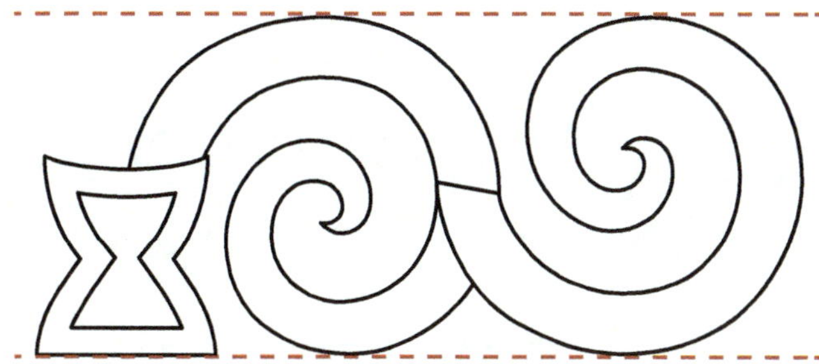

Keep adding curls until the design fills the length you need. Always make sure to reverse the curls on the vine for a natural look. If the first curl is clockwise the next should be counterclockwise, and so on.

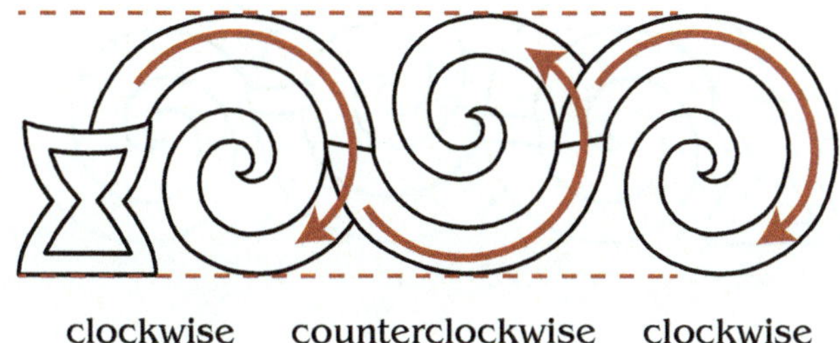

Once all your curls are in place, you'll want to finesse your joins. The two can simply be merged together into a single branching strand.

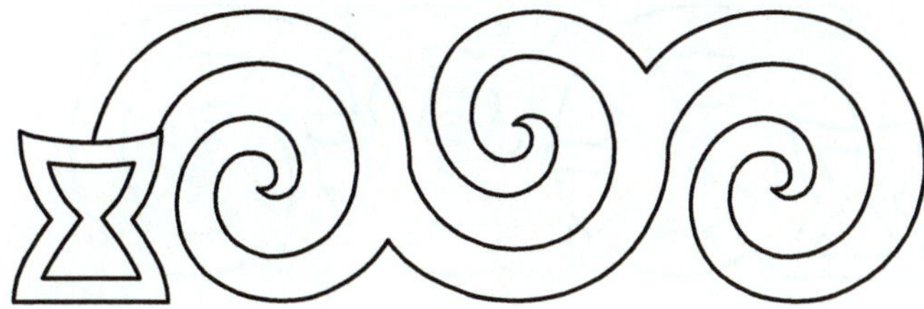

Vine & Chalice...

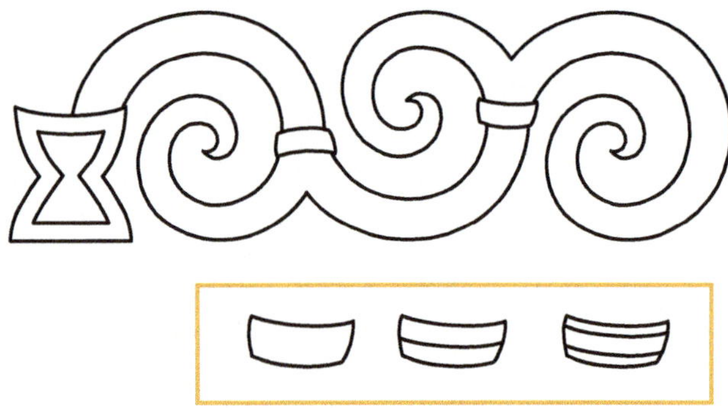

Commonly, each curl springs from a band shape when the vine splits. This band can be left plain or decorated with inside stripes.

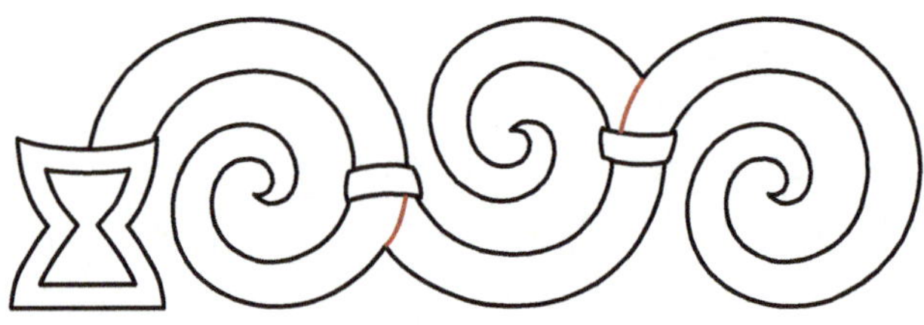

To add some extra detail and give the illusion of three dimensions, we can split the vines from where they spring from the band by adding a small curve from the band up to the split in the vine. If you examine the vine curls where they split, you'll see that one appears to be the final wee bit from the previous strand finishing up, and the other is the thicker strand of the new vine curl beginning. Add the curve so the new big curl looks as if it is "in front of" the smaller one.

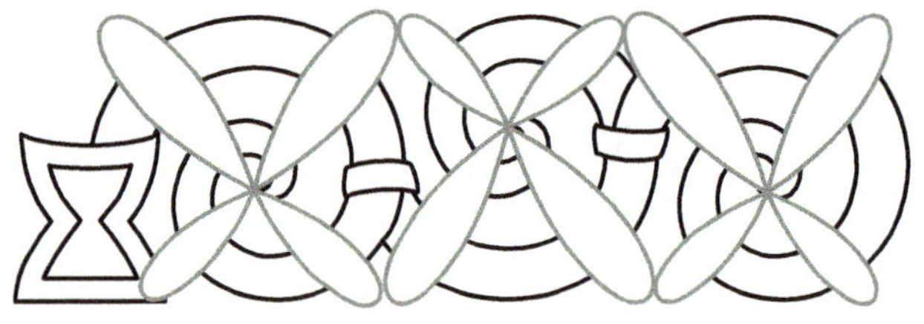

Our leaves are basically a teardrop shape coming from the tips of our vine curls. They are added in sets of either 3 or 4, depending on your design and what room you have. Pencil the leaves in lightly, making sure there's room for every leaf tip. Leaves should fit neatly within the overall design.

Vine & Chalice...

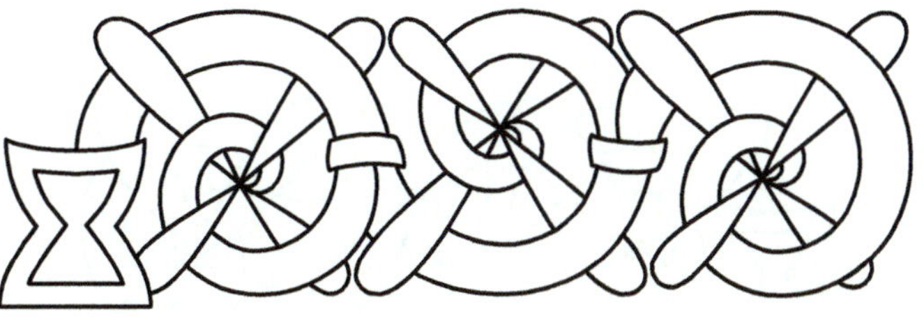

Next, weave the leaves into the vine tendrils. Starting with the vine where it emerges from the chalice, weave the tendril under and then over each leaf it encounters in an alternating pattern of under-over-under-over. Continue this pattern with the new tendrils as they spring from the old tendrils at the bands, until all the leaves are woven in.

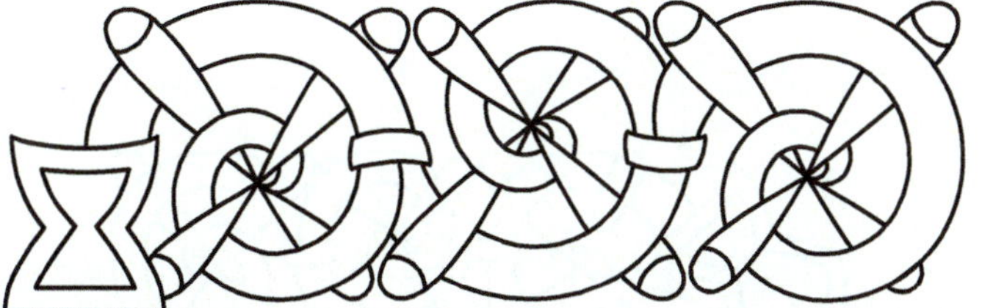

Add one last bit of decoration to the leaves, with a little scoop or dot at each tip (where they show in the overs and unders). This creates one more part to color differently in the final artwork and adds extra detail.

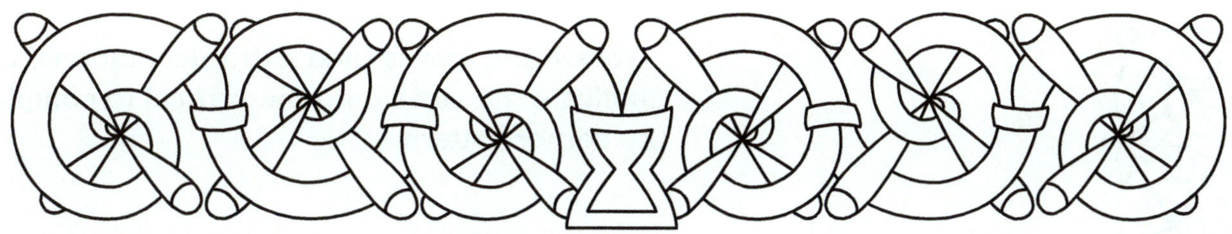

For the final step, duplicate the design on the left-hand side, so the entire horizontal border is complete.

Vine & Chalice...

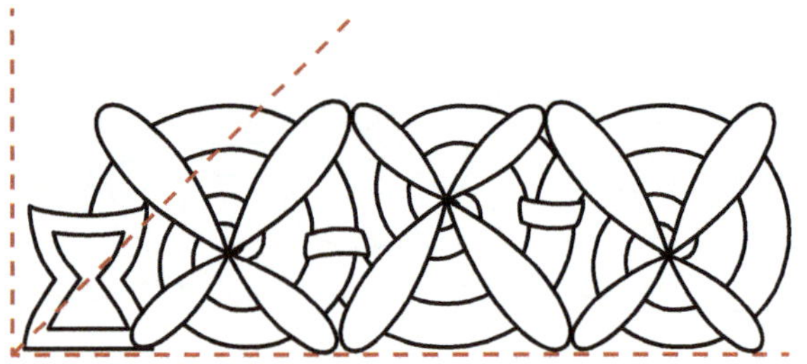

Deriving a corner design from the horizontal design is fairly easy, and involves the same steps in just a slightly different format.

Notice how half of the horizontal design almost fits within a corner format.

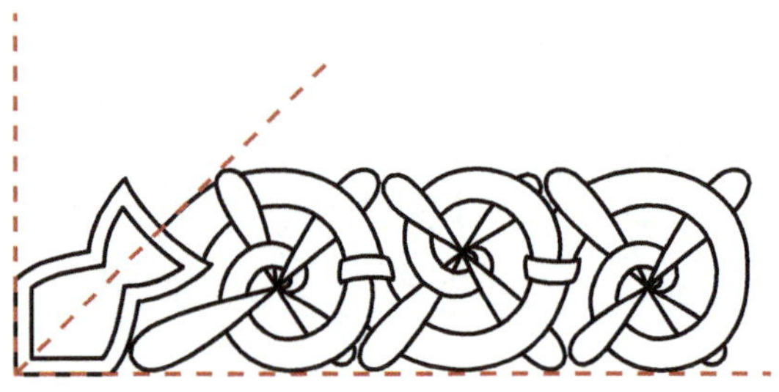

By tilting the chalice so it sits at 45 degrees with the corner and tweaking the vines as they emerge from the chalice, the horizontal design easily fits into a corner format.

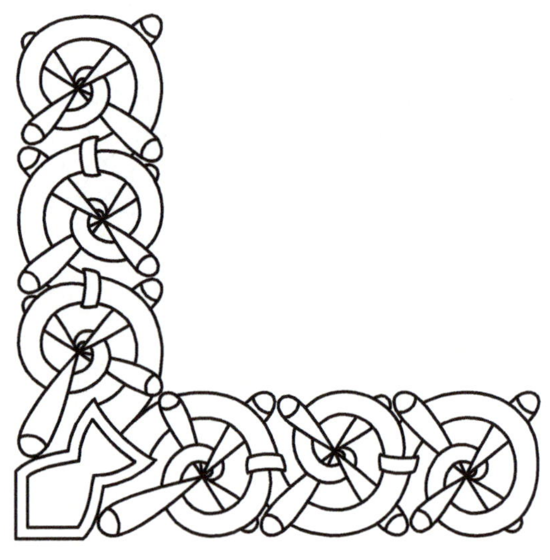

Weave the leaves, add extra decorations, and duplicate the vines onto the vertical to complete the corner pattern.

Vine & Chalice...

A vertical version of the previous design is easy to create, but now that we know the basics let's experiment with a more natural-looking vine.

In this style, the vine stem branches and curves from side to side in a more natural manner and leaves more open space for adding leaves, decorative elements, or even animals. Begin by creating your chalice and determining the width and length of your overall design.

With that in place, add the beginnings of the vine, starting with its main central branch. The branch should rise from the chalice, undulating from side to side, with its width slowly tapering as it reaches the tip.

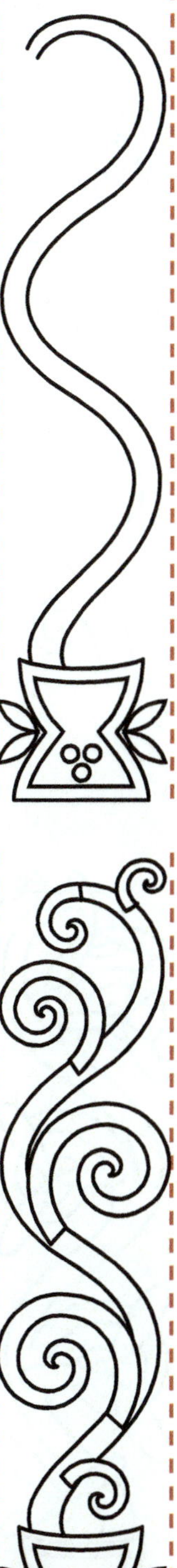

From the main stem, add curls, using them to fill the spaces left by the main stem. I also vary the size of the curls in the example to the right, so in general they begin larger at the bottom near the chalice and then become smaller at the top. I've added a few small ones here and there to fill in empty spaces, and added a curly tip to the very top of my main stem.

Vine & Chalice...

Next, I merge the vine curls with the main vine stem. This time they appear as natural joins, rather than adding the band where they branch or split.

There is a lot of flexibility at this point. The curling tendrils can be left as is, we can add some leaves, or we can even translate the design into waves pouring from a cup, or smoke emerging from a cauldron.

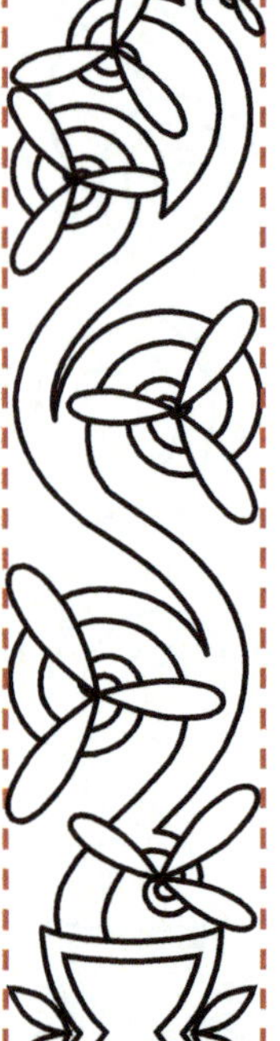

In keeping with the plant motif, add some leaves. Don't forget that along with the traditional Celtic vine leaves, it's possible to use any leaf from any tree or plant as a model.

I use the same leaf set as before in the example, but feel free to experiment with your own designs.

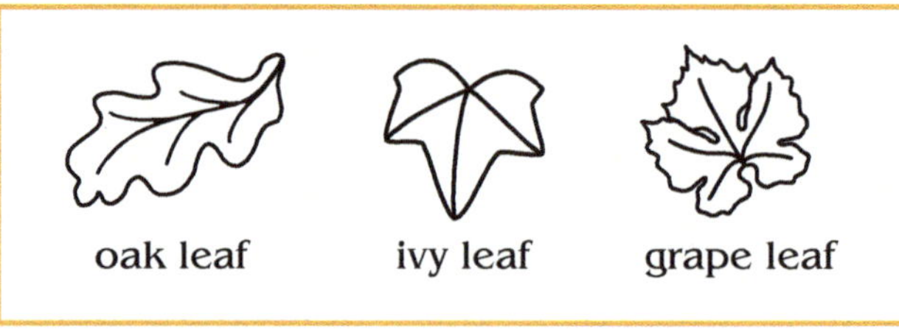

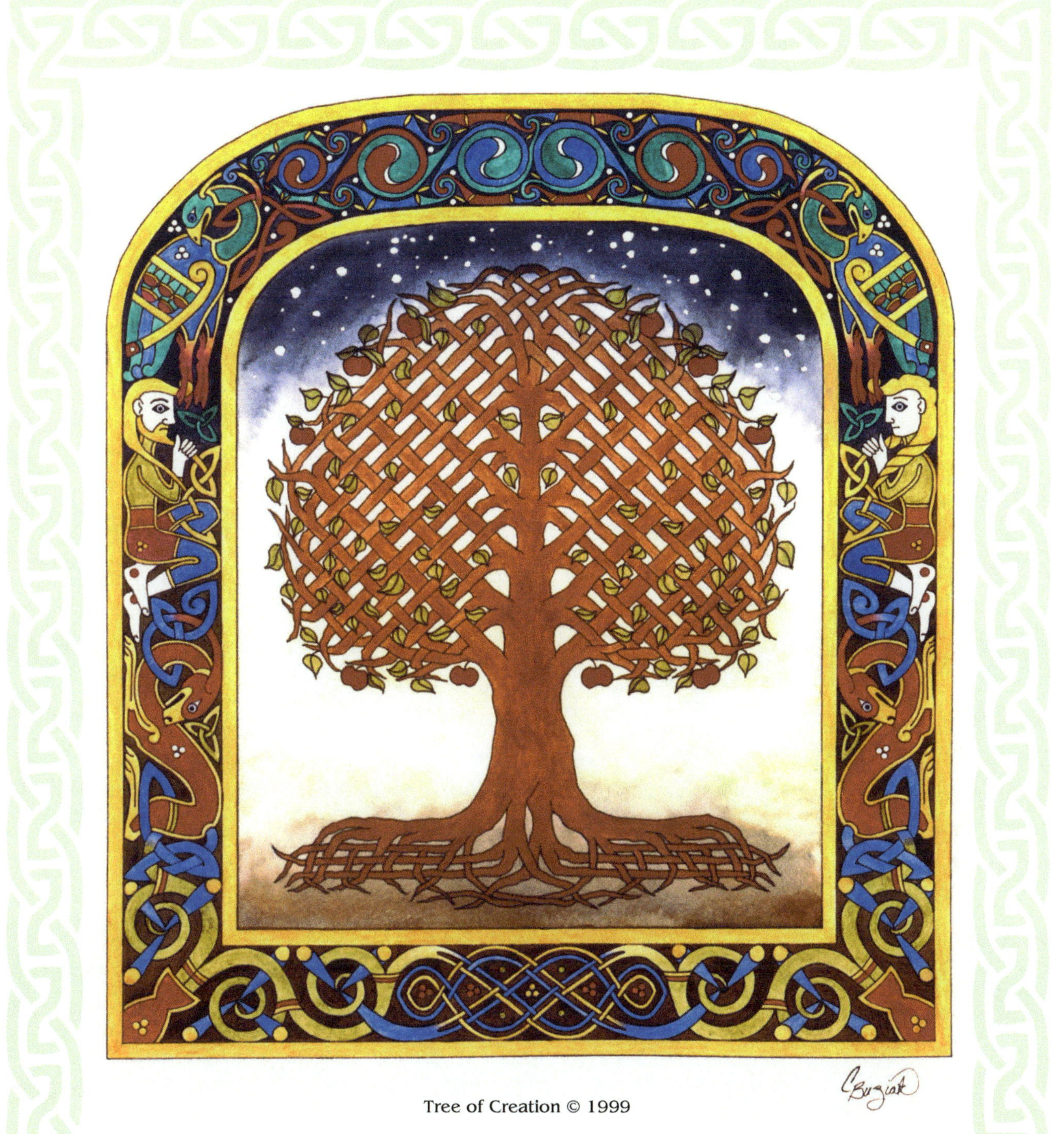

Tree of Creation © 1999

TECHNIQUES & MATERIALS

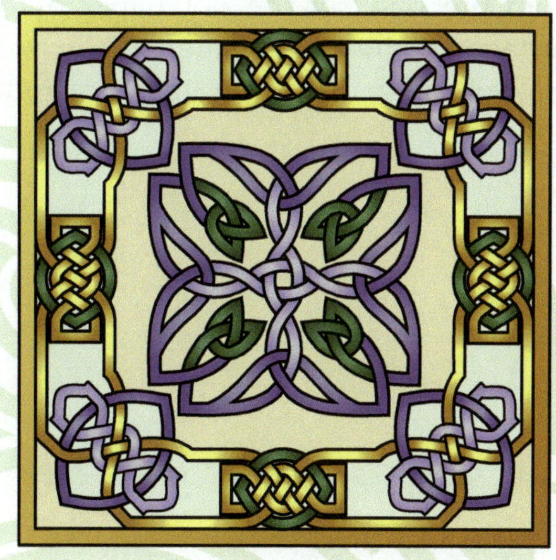

Techniques

Transferring a design

There are two tricks you can use to transfer a finished design from the dotted paper to good paper.

In the first method, take the dot paper and flip it over so the back side is facing up. Take a good old-fashioned hand-sharpened pencil (mechanical ones don't work as well for this), and tilt it on its side so the exposed graphite lays on the paper. Then shade the back of your dot paper. It's not necessary to cover the whole area, just the areas underneath the design. Check if you missed anything by holding the page up to a window; the light will show where you've missed shading. Once the back is covered, flip the sheet over again and position it over the good paper. It can be helpful to use low-tack masking tape or blue painter's tape to hold down the dot paper to the good paper so it doesn't move.

Now take a ballpoint pen and trace over your design. Press as lightly as possible because you don't want to emboss the outlines into the good paper below. The pressure from the pen transfers the graphite from the back of the dot paper onto the surface of the good paper. When you lift the dot paper away the lines are redrawn on the good paper, ready for painting and erasable if necessary.

The second method is less messy. Buy a sheet of transfer paper from the art store that has the graphite already on it. You use this paper in between your dot paper and your good paper, almost as you would use a sheet of carbon paper. You can reuse this sheet many times before you have to get a new one. The paper may be called "transfer paper" or "graphite paper", and sometimes it even comes in colors! White transfer paper is very useful when transferring onto a darker paper because it's more visible.

Tip

Before tracing the entire design, do a small section then lift a corner of your sheet up. Make sure that you're pressing hard enough to transfer the design, but not so hard that you damage the paper, before continuing. Better to have to re-do a corner than the whole design if you find it's not transferring well!

Materials

Pen and Ink

"Pen and Ink" can mean a lot of different things and it's a medium that can be utilized with a lot of different materials. For this discussion, we'll assume that this is for good works meant to be kept, framed, sold, or given away. You can draw your Celtic knots with anything, but some materials are more archival than others, meaning that they will last longer. The ink from some pens (such as ballpoints) will fade or change color over time, and some papers (such as newsprint) will yellow and become brittle. This may not matter if you're only sketching, but if you want to make something that will look good 10 years down the road you need to choose more archival materials. Most of these materials are available at art or craft stores.

Pens

The traditional type of pen used for Pen and Ink is a dip-style pen. As with old-fashioned calligraphy pens, you purchase the nib for the pen and the body separately. The nibs come in a variety of sizes, and should be chosen depending on the detail you want on your final piece. Some popular types are the Hawk and the Crow quills. The constant dipping of the pen into ink can be messy and cumbersome, but these quills are excellent for making outlines in colors other than black because you choose whatever color ink you want.

You can also use pigment-based pens that are like tiny felt pens, but are of archival quality. These pens are also waterproof when dry. They won't fade (unlike a dye-based marker), and they come in several different tip sizes, helpful depending on the size of detail you're doing. I prefer these over pretty much anything, and use different-sized tips for different parts of each painting, whether it's a tiny detail or a border outline, etc.

Inks

Many colored inks are dye based, so be careful when you buy the ink. Check with sales staff or read the product information sheet to see if the ink you pick is light fast. If it is not light fast, over time the color will fade or change.

You can also get colored inks that are pigment based, meaning that some colors are resistant to fading. Depending on the pigment, some colors will still fade, but overall with pigmented inks there may be a color option that will work for you and also will not fade. Look for a chart or product information sheet that describes which colors are light fast, moderately light fast, or not light fast at all.

A common version of pigment-based inks is liquid acrylics. These have the same properties as regular acrylic paints (large range of colors, waterproof when dry) except that they're very thin and runny rather than pasty.

As far as a standard black ink goes, there are many versions you can choose from. Usually these will be labeled as calligraphy inks. If you're going to be coloring the insides of your knots, choose a waterproof ink to outline them, so the outside lines don't run when you're coloring the interiors.

Paper

Papers chosen for Pen and Ink are usually smooth because of the detail involved. A very rough paper is difficult to make a nice straight line on—it tends to wiggle around.

There are also handmade papers with bits of leaves, petals, and bark in them that produce nice effects. Always test your ink on a scrap of paper to see how much the ink will bleed.

Watercolor paper is another option, especially if you want to stain the background or use watercolor paints on it after you've finished outlining. Watercolor paper is very heavy, and good quality watercolor paper is archival. It comes in different levels of smoothness and thickness (weight), so choose what's appropriate for your project.

Acrylics

Acrylic Paints

Acrylics can be used thick and straight from the tube or thinned with water or a thinning medium. All acrylics are waterproof once dry and can be cleaned up with regular soap and water. If you want to use your acrylics very thin and runny, you may want to look into a liquid acrylic (see the Pen and Ink section on page 109) to save yourself time.

Artist quality is the best, but student-quality acrylic paints are more affordable. Both come in many bright colors.

Acrylic Paint Surfaces

Acrylics can be used on pretty much any surface, from wood to paper to leather. I've used acrylics to paint suede bookcovers, on wood, and I often use them on paper because they are so waterproof. It's best to use a very heavy paper with acrylics or else thin the paint for use on lighter papers. When acrylic paint is used full strength on a light paper, it makes the paper curl and pucker.

Canvas boards are available to paint on, but they usually have a weave texture to them so they don't work as well for small intricate images. These and stretched canvases (canvas stretched around a wooden frame) are great, however, for large works, because the details will also be large enough not to be distorted by the canvas texture.

Acrylic paints work well on watercolor paper. Try to get a paper with a weight between 140lb or 300lb. You can also find watercolor paper mounted on stiff backing board (PK Board is an example), which is the best of both worlds—a watercolor surface with a stiff backing.

Materials...

Watercolors

Watercolor Paints

Watercolors come as a paste in a tiny tube or as a dried puck of paint. They are used diluted and are not waterproof. If you make a mistake while painting in watercolor, you can wait for the spot to dry thoroughly and then take a stiff, damp brush and scrub the spot out carefully, taking care not to damage the paper.

Watercolors can be cleaned up with regular soap and water. If you want to work with watercolor on top of pen and ink, make sure that the ink you use to outline is waterproof. If you want to be able to place layer upon layer of color without disturbing previous layers, you may want to look into liquid acrylics instead (see the Pen and Ink section on page 109). It will provide similar results but because it dries waterproof you will be able to paint subsequent layers overtop without redissolving the previous layers.

Watercolors, like acrylics, come in different qualities. Student quality is usually not as concentrated or as pure as artist quality; however, choosing good student-quality paint can be an economical way to purchase a variety of colors, and often come in sets. Also, if you've mixed a specific color on your palette you can let it dry and re-wet it the next day to use again!

Paper

Watercolor paper is available in different formats. It can come in a pad (like a regular sketch pad), a block (where the sheets are glued all around the pad on the edges), or single full-sized sheets. If you plan on working very wet and soaking your paper, you may want to use single sheets and stretch the paper before use so it won't buckle. A nice alternative to this is the watercolor block. The blocks are glued around the edges and you paint straight onto the top sheet of the block. The glue holds the sheet flat while you work and any buckling usually straightens out once you let the sheet dry attached to the block. Remove the sheet from the block after the painting is finished and has completely dried.

Watercolor pads usually come in 140lb weight, although sometimes you may be able to find 90lb. Either is acceptable, but if you're not sure how wet you'll be painting, get the 140lb. It's better to have it too heavy than too light, and risk wrinkling as you paint.

Single sheets come in a standard size of 22″ x 30″ and are available in standard weights of 90lb, 140lb, and 300lb. If you're working very wet consider the 300lb so you don't have to worry about the paper buckling as much, or having to stretch it.

Watercolor paper also comes in different textures—smooth (Hot Pressed), medium (Cold Pressed) or rough (Rough). The most common is the Cold Pressed texture. Hot Pressed is used for paintings with finer detail and Rough is used to add some visible texture to a particular piece. Full-size sheets may be purchased and then cut down to the size needed. Choose what works best for your individual projects.

Biography

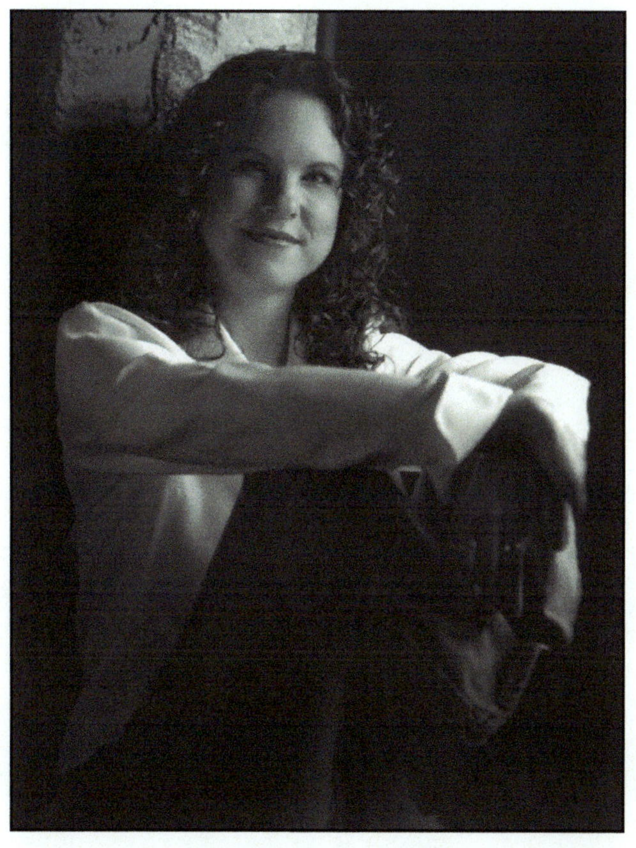

Cari Buziak currently lives in Calgary, Alberta, with one cat, one dog, and one beehive. She enjoys crafting and creating costumes and doing all sorts of creative things like knitting and quilting. In a mix of old techniques (handmade gesso, egg tempera, gold leaf) and new (several Mac computers) she recreates ancient manuscripts in painted and digital form for a wide variety of merchandising and fine art needs.

Idolized artists include Jon Muth, Charles Vess, Brian Froud, Maxfield Parrish, and Archibald Knox. In the summer of 2000, Cari had the honor of being invited to Ireland to work as the artist for an archaeology dig. The Ballykilcline Project, centered in Strokestown, County Roscommon, gave her the opportunity to reconstruct artifacts by sketching, create promotional paintings of the dig site, and also to further her own research into Celtic art and mythology.

Current and past published works include book illustrations for Dover Publications, Interweave Press, Penguin/Pearson Books, Llewellyn Publications, and Chronicle Books; designing for Irish Dance dresses, jewelry designs, and other commissioned works. Her work has been featured in design magazines and she has had gallery exhibitions in Calgary, Toronto, Indiana, Florida, Michigan, Wisconsin, Oregon, Japan, London, and New York. Cari has sold worldwide and her artwork appears in private collections in Canada, Europe, Japan, and the United States.

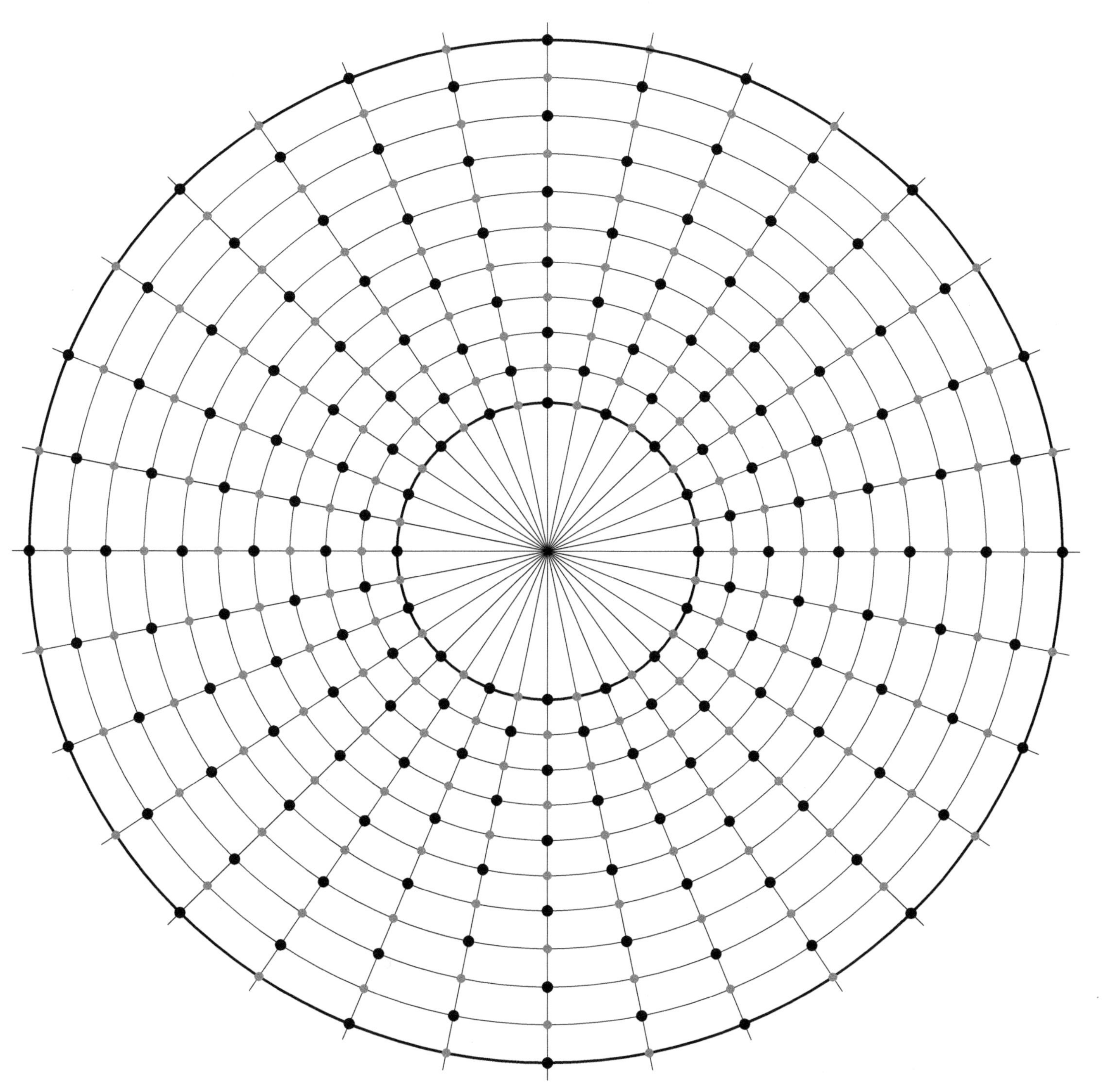